PRINT'S BEST BOOKLETS & BROCHURES

PRINT'S BEST BOOKLETS & BROCHURES

Library of Congress Catalog Card Number 94-067218
ISBN 0-915734-94-X

RC PUBLICATIONS

President and Publisher: Howard Cadel
Vice President and Editor: Martin Fox
Creative Director: Andrew Kner
Managing Director, Book Projects: Linda Silver
Administrative Assistant: Nancy Silver
Assistant Art Director: Michele L. Trombley

BOOKLETS & BROCHURES

WINNING DESIGNS FROM PRINT MAGAZINE'S NATIONAL COMPETITION

Edited by
LINDA SILVER

Introduction by
POPPY EVANS

Designed by
ANDREW KNER

Published by
RC PUBLICATIONS, INC.
NEW YORK, NY

The publications showcased in this book represent state-of-the-art design in booklet and brochure format. Selected from thousands of entries submitted to PRINT magazine's Regional Design Annual, all were deemed winners by the editors and art director of PRINT. This book allows us to devote more space to these selections and facilitates a better understanding of their design through display of pages and covers as well as selected details.

As you look at the booklets and brochures featured in this book, the versatility of this multi-page format will be self-evident. Brochures serve a variety of communication needs in a broad range of sizes, formats and stylistic treatments. Regardless of scope of purpose and style, all of these pieces have one thing in common: They convey a message of considerable length through a series of pages, and they accomplish this through powerful design. Taking a large body of information and organizing it in a logical and reader-friendly manner is no small feat in itself. Making it into a publication that will engage an individual as well as persuade, inform and even prompt the reader to action is effective communication design at its best.

What makes a great brochure? Whether it's a catalog, a capabilities brochure, or a product or promotional brochure, effective publication design begins with a great cover. A brochure with a dynamic cover will immediately engage the observer, beguiling him or her to browse through its pages. If it appears on a shelf among other brochures,

CONTENTS

a great cover will call attention to itself, signalling that the publication it encases is something special.

Beyond the cover, a brochure's interior pages will guide the reader through its message from beginning to end. Information is logically organized and hierarchy established through strategic use of headlines and subheads. Copy is alternated with visuals which add impact and further enhance the brochure's message.

Type, color and other graphic elements work together harmoniously to visually unify a brochure's pages. Graphic themes and their variations create an overall impression and help to establish an image which will promote the desired perception of an organization's product or service.

However, the ultimate test of a brochure's effectiveness is how it performs in the hands of its intended audience. Just as a widget catalog must sell widgets, a capabilities brochure must clearly promote an organization's accomplishments. It must be easy to read as well as easy on the eye, and it must fully engage its recipients to the point where they understand and even consider acting on its message.

Whether they are selling a product or promoting an image, the brochures featured in this book do their job, each achieving its communication goal while maintaining the highest design standards. The complexities involved in designing and producing each makes our appreciation of this body of work that much greater.—*Poppy Evans*

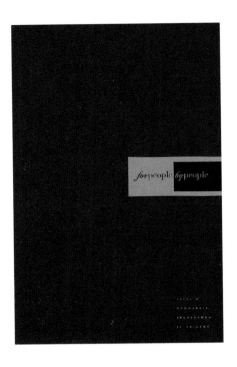

Promotional package designed to communicate the corporation's awareness of, and responsibility to, the community and the environment.

DESIGN FIRM:
Vaughn/Wedeen Creative, Albuquerque, New Mexico

ART DIRECTOR/
DESIGNER: Steve Wedeen

COMPUTER PRODUCTION:

Heather Scanlon

PHOTOGRAPHER:

Sue Bennett

COPYWRITER:

Nathan James

QUANTITY: 5000

PRINTING PROCESS:

Offset

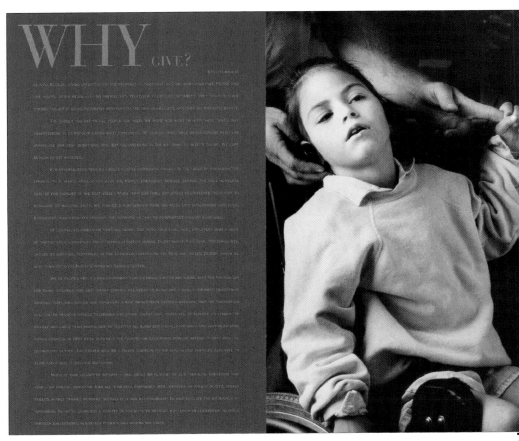

Self-promotion.

DESIGN FIRM:

Baker Design Associates,

Santa Monica, California

ART DIRECTOR/

DESIGNER/

PHOTOGRAPHER:

Gary Robert Baker

BUDGET: $40,000

QUANTITY: 3000

PRINTING PROCESS:

Lithography

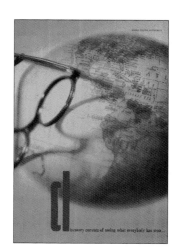

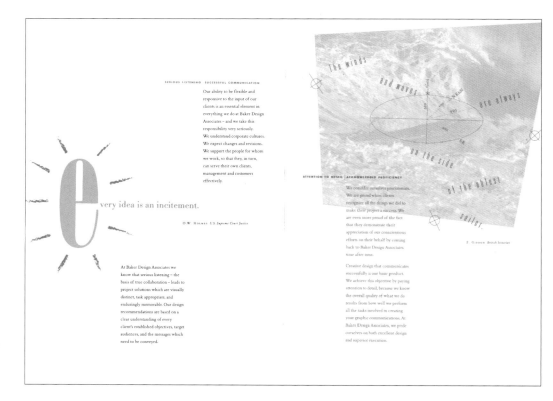

Baker Design Associates

Labor-issues brochure, part of a series of brochures designed to explain economic principles to high school students.

DESIGN FIRM:
Linda Helton Design, Dallas, Texas

DESIGNER/ILLUSTRATOR:
Linda Helton

TYPOGRAPHY:
Mouseworks

QUANTITY: 12,000

PRINTING PROCESS:
6 PMS colors (Labor, The Economy & Monetary Policy), 4-color plus 1 PMS plus varnish (International Trade and the Economy)

Federal Reserve Bank of Dallas

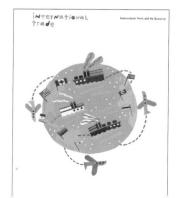

Left: covers of two other brochures in the series.

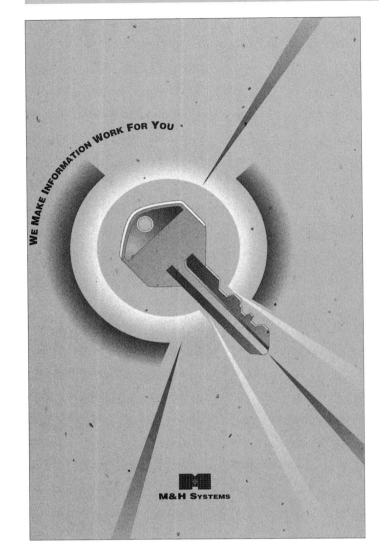

WE MAKE INFORMATION WORK FOR YOU

M&H SYSTEMS

Capabilities brochure for a provider of management information systems for the petrochemical industry.
DESIGN FIRM: Piland/Goodell, Inc., Houston, Texas
DESIGNER: Don Goodell
ILLUSTRATORS: David Piland, Paul Hera
COPYWRITER: Steve Barnhill

BETTER DATA ACCESS CAN PRODUCE FAR-REACHING BENEFITS

At M&H, we transform information into convenient, cost-efficient management resources. Freeing you to work faster and smarter. And enabling you to be more effective.

At your request, we sift through data you have, eliminate what you don't need, and create a library of information that becomes a tool with far-reaching power and immediate usefulness in such specific areas as

    Maintenance tracking
    Document management
    Production administration
    Compliance management
    Training programs
    Financial management
    Contractor management
    And other executive functions.

And we do it all with popular, widely available programming tools. So costs and complications are kept to an absolute minimum.

FIFTEEN YEARS' EXPERIENCE SHAPES EVERYTHING WE DO

Our experience in information management spans more than 15 years. It includes systems analysis, high-level programming and multimedia tool creation, hardware and software troubleshooting, long-term support, upgrades and expansion for systems we have created.

Already, the M&H information systems in operation include:

Offshore Oil & Gas Production Information Gathering Systems. M&H-created systems are recording daily oil and gas production, sea conditions, and weather for worldwide fleets, linked with onshore servers.

Personnel Management Systems. Our systems are tracking employee tenure, training, salary and other facets of personnel work histories.

Equipment Maintenance Systems. M&H information systems are planning and scheduling equipment maintenance, generating work orders and reports, tracking costs, parts in inventory — all strategically linked to mainframe accounting systems.

Electronic Performance Support Systems. Our multimedia EPS Systems are making compliance with OSHA 29 CFR 1910 pay dividends for client companies.

Document Management Systems. M&H systems are automating the bureaucratic documentation of Process Safety Management and other "paper - heavy" processes.

Capabilities brochure.

DESIGN FIRM:

Ema Design,

Denver, Colorado

ART DIRECTOR:

Thomas C. Ema

DESIGNER:

Debra Johnson Humphrey

PHOTOGRAPHER:

Allen Kennedy

PRINTER:

Communigraphics

BUDGET: $18,000

QUANTITY: 5000

PRINTING PROCESS:

Lithography

MCC Construction Corporation (Construction/Renovation/Repair)

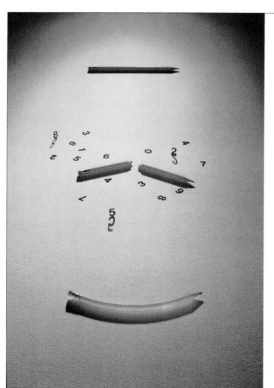

MONEY

MCC Construction Corporation's Delivery Order Contracting system (MCC DOC) is the shortest and sanest distance between contracting starts and finishes. By streamlining all phases of maintenance, renovation and construction, it eliminates the wear and tear on your budget, time and nerves.

MCC was one of the prime contractors selected when the Department of Defense originally implemented Delivery Order Contracting (DOC) to reduce delays and cut costs on Army and Air Force bases. Two programs were developed — SABER (Simplified Acquisition of Base Engineering Requirements) for the Air Force and JOC (Job Order Contracting) for the Army. These programs have resulted in lead time reductions of 50% to 75% and cost savings of 15% to 20%.

In addition to being one of the main participating contractors for SABER and JOC, MCC contributed to further developments and refinements of the concept. Our dedication to proving the value of DOC to each and every client has made us one of the top JOC and SABER contractors in the nation.

Two important features of our DOC system is a unit price book and a fixed profit and overhead percentage. Based on the Means database and including some 37,000 line items, our unit price book is tailored to reflect prices in your locale. The unit price book takes the mystery out of contracting costs and enables you to effectively control costs by specifying the level of quality desired for materials. The fixed profit and overhead percentage limits how much MCC can make on any one project. For the life of your contract with MCC, the same percentage is added to the total line items of each estimate.

Under pressure to keep costs down and results up, consider flexing your pencil with MCC's Delivery Order Contracting system.

The fundamental things apply as time goes by.

JAZZ COMPOSITION

You have plans for your music. There is a glorious tradition in jazz that needs you to add your thread to the pattern. Ellington, Miles, and Mingus left, but they left us richer. Now it's your turn. With what you have heard from the past and know about the present, you'll write music that will take us off into the future. You are getting the tools in class and you keep listening to everybody, but you are making very sure that you listen closely to yourself.

MUSIC PRODUCTION & ENGINEERING

Problem solving is your forte: whether it's working out a perfect mix or smoothing out a miscommunication between the musicians and the technical crew. You're both a creator with a golden ear and a collaborator who finds common ground for all the players involved with a music production. There's something else you want to say in addition to what you compose or what comes out of your instrument. And that's what comes out of your imagination.

When you were seven, you had this incredible piano teacher. She wanted you to like piano, so she didn't make you play little kids' songs or just the classical stuff. First she said, "What do you like to listen to?" You told her you liked rock and folk music. So she got you a "Fake Book," and you started with Little Feat's "Time Loves a Hero." She told you that your parents would like that just as much as "Moonlight Sonata" if you played it really well. Maybe more.

MUSIC EDUCATION

As a teacher, live is when you reach for the stars and you get it.

VISITING ARTISTS

Prospectus.

DESIGN FIRM:

Moore Moscowitz, Brookline, Massachusetts

ART DIRECTORS:

Tim Moore, Jan Moscowitz

DESIGNER: Tim Moore

PHOTOGRAPHERS:

Clark Quin, Michele McDonald, Russell Monk

ILLUSTRATORS:

Lee Busch, Erik Adigard

QUANTITY: 40,000

PRINTING PROCESS: 5/5 offset lithography

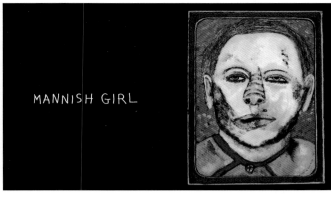

MANNISH GIRL

THE UNIDENTIFIED WOMAN

THE NEW DRESS

NOW I HAVE THE FAN

William Traver Gallery (Art Gallery)

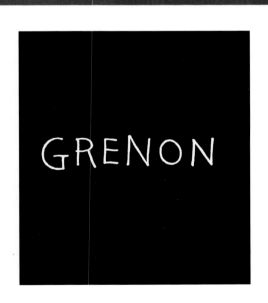

GRENON

Promotional catalog for a show of the work of Gregory Grenon.

AGENCY:

The Traver Company, Seattle, Washington

ART DIRECTOR:

Anne Traver

DESIGNERS: Anne Traver, Kristine Matthews

PHOTOGRAPHER:

Bill Bachhuber

The Imaginary Life of Claude Monet

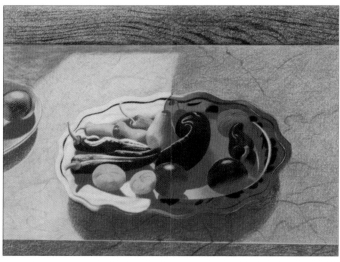

Milton Glaser, Inc./Toppan Printing Co.

Booklet on Impressionist painter Claude Monet; joint self-promotion for designer and printer.
DESIGN FIRM: Milton Glaser Inc., New York, New York
ART DIRECTOR/ DESIGNER/ILLUSTRATOR: Milton Glaser

COPYWRITER: Shirley Glaser
SEPARATOR/PRINTER/ BINDER: Toppan Printing Co. (America), Inc.
QUANTITY: 2000
PRINTING PROCESS: 4-color plus two matched colors

Direct-mail catalog.

AGENCY:

Moffatt & Rosenthal,

Lake Oswego, Oregon

ART DIRECTOR/

DESIGNER:

Kurt D. Hollomon

ILLUSTRATORS:

Jack A. Molloy, Vivienne

Flesher, George Cheney

Mackenzie River Co. (Sport Fishing Clothing)

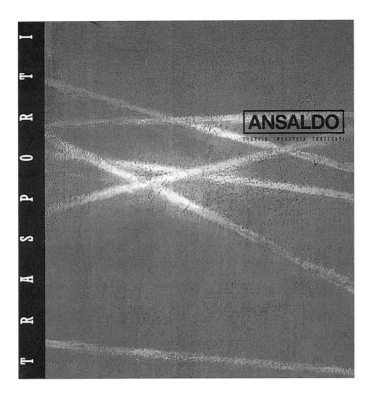

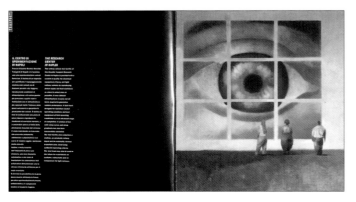

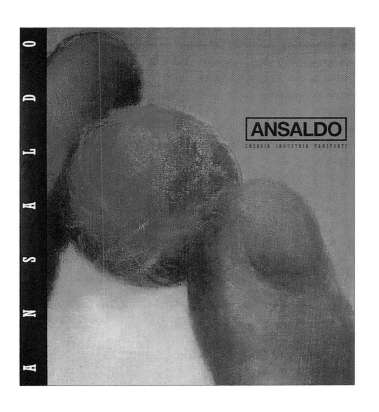

ANSALDO

ANSALDO
ENERGIA INDUSTRIA TRASPORTI

A series of capabilities brochures for the various independent units of an electromechanical engineering group.

ILLUSTRATOR:

Brad Holland,

New York, New York

AGENCY:

J. Walter Thompson/Milan

ART DIRECTOR:

Claudia Brambilla

Ansaldo Transporti Research Center

LA RICERCA MOTORE DELL'INNOVAZIONE
RESEARCH THE DRIVING FORCE BEHIND INNOVATION

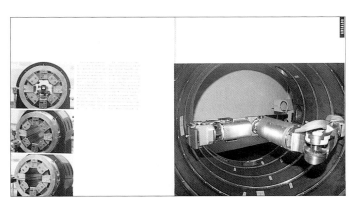

RAGGIO D'AZIONE IL MONDO
MARKETPLACE THE WORLD

ENERGIE ALTERNATIVE
ALTERNATIVE POWER

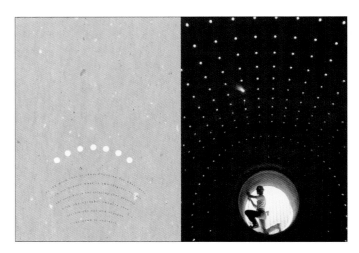

Tejada Photography

Self-promotion.

DESIGN FIRM:

Ema Design,

Denver, Colorado

ART DIRECTOR:

Thomas C. Ema

DESIGNER:

Debra Johnson Humphrey

PHOTOGRAPHER:

David Tejada

PRINTER:

Communigraphics

BUDGET: $8000

QUANTITY: 1000

PRINTING PROCESS:

Lithography

"*The camera never lies*" stopped being a truism long before Macintosh design and programs like ImageStudio came along. Realistic depictions of the absurd, like Michael Houghton's pencils high as doorways, force viewers to rethink their perceptions. In some printers' hands, such depictions might be taken for mistakes rather than statements. At Baesman we pride ourselves on knowing the difference.

Printed in four color process with an overall dry trap gloss varnish

Color and the demand for color — in television, in newspapers, in virtually every medium — so saturates our culture, that photographers like Tom Watson can employ black and white photography to express what process color cannot. Black and white's relative simplicity enables a designer to color the vision that a photographer discovers. And it lets the people at Baesman reveal the artistry of both.

Tritone printed in process black and two PMS greys with an overall dry trap gloss varnish

Baesman Printing (Color Printer)

Promotional brochure.

AGENCY:

Rickabaugh Graphics, Gahanna, Ohio

ART DIRECTORS:

Rod Baseman, Eric Rickabaugh

DESIGNER:

Michael Tennyson Smith

PHOTOGRAPHERS:

D.R. Goff, Tom Watson, Larry Hamil, Paul Poplis, Chas Krider

COPYWRITER:

John Hofmeister

QUANTITY: 1000

PRINTING PROCESS:

Offset lithography

GTE Directories (Telephone Book Publisher)

On-Call Information
Services promotion
targeting business clients.
DESIGN FIRM:
Sullivan Perkins,
Dallas, Texas
ART DIRECTOR: Art Garcia
DESIGNERS/
ILLUSTRATORS:
Art Garcia,
Lorraine Charman
COPYWRITER:
Mark Perkins
PRINTER:
Yaquinto Printing Co., Inc.
PRINTING PROCESS:
4-color plus gloss varnish
plus dull varnish

Promotion for a line of

shoes.

ART DIRECTOR/

DESIGNER: Robert Lussier/

Kenneth Cole,

New York, New York

PHOTOGRAPHER:

Carlton Davis

COPYWRITER:

Leslie Herman

Prospectus/course
catalog.
DESIGN FIRM:
Stoltze Design,
Boston , Massachusetts
ART DIRECTOR:
Clifford Stoltze
DESIGNERS: Kyong Choe,
Clifford Stoltze, Peter
Farrell, Rebecca Fagan

BUDGET: $79,860
QUANTITY: 30,000
PRINTING PROCESS:
Offset

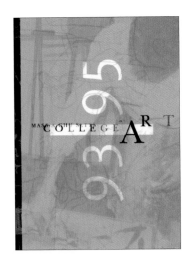

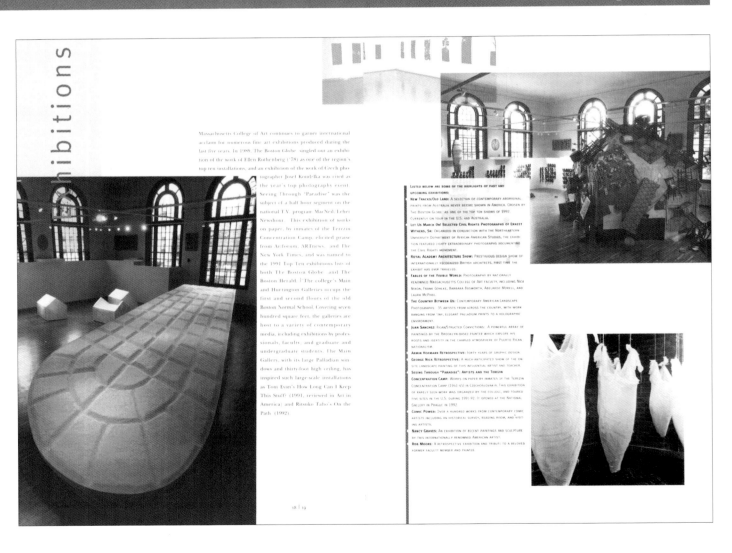

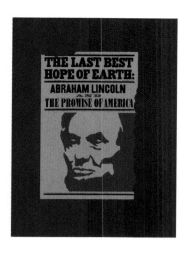

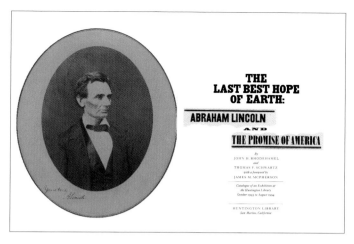

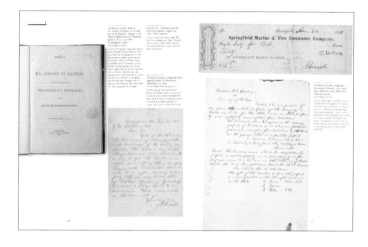

Catalog for a Lincoln exhibit.

DESIGN FIRM:
Ken Parkhurst & Associates,
Los Angeles, California

ART DIRECTOR:
Ken Parkhurst

DESIGNER:
Denis Parkhurst

PHOTOGRAPHERS:
Bob Schlosser,
John Sullivan

ILLUSTRATOR:
Gina Bessire

BUDGET: $42,000
(including typography and separations)

QUANTITY: 40,000

PRINTING PROCESS:
Offset lithography donated by Nestlé U.S.A.,
Print Services Division

We take great pleasure in bringing you **Elmore James—King Of The Slide Guitar—The Fire/Fury/Enjoy Recordings,** the latest installment in our "Capricorn Records Presents" series.

This package salutes the great Elmore James during the year of his induction into the Rock and Roll Hall of Fame. He is one of a handful of guitarists whose style and sound remain instantly recognizable, influencing several generations of guitar players.

Elmore James has been a profound influence on many Capricorn artists through the years, none more so than The Allman Brothers Band, who covered his "Done Somebody Wrong" on their classic live album, **At Fillmore East;** paid homage to James's take on "One Way Out" on their **Eat A Peach** album, and used Elmore's classic lament, "The Sky Is Crying," to bid farewell to Duane Allman at his funeral.

Under the guidance of producer/songwriter and record company executive Bobby Robinson, Elmore James recorded his most creative and explosive sides during the years he spent on Robinson's Fire/Fury/Enjoy labels from 1959 to 1963. Although his four-year association with Fire/Fury/Enjoy would end prematurely because of his death from a heart attack, the music Elmore James left behind on these recordings is a powerful testament to his continued importance in contemporary American music.

**Phil Walden, President
Capricorn Records**

"I practiced twelve hours a day, every day, until my fingers were bleeding, trying to get the same sound as Elmore James. This went on for weeks and weeks, and finally someone told me, 'He plays with a slide.'"

—Robbie Robertson, at the 1992 Rock and Roll Hall of Fame Induction Ceremony honoring Elmore James

CD booklet and packaging.

ART DIRECTOR:
Kim Champagne/
Warner Bros. Records,
Burbank, California
DESIGNERS:
Kim Champagne,
Mike Diehl (booklet)
ILLUSTRATOR:
Josh Gosfield
BUDGET: $10,000
QUANTITY: 10,000
PRINTING PROCESS:
4-color, sheet-fed offset

Promotional package for 45th anniversary of association of West Coast fraternity and sorority leaders.

DESIGN FIRM:

Sayles Graphic Design,

Des Moines, Iowa

DESIGNER: John Sayles

COPYWRITER:

Sheree Clark

QUANTITY: 2000

PRINTING PROCESS:

2-color offset

Promotion for a clothing
line.

DESIGN FIRM: Toth, Inc.,
Concord, Massachusetts
ART DIRECTOR/
DESIGNER:
Michael C. Toth
PHOTOGRAPHER:
Bruce Weber
BUDGET: $80,000
QUANTITY: 20,000
PRINTING PROCESS:
Lithography

Pepe Jeans

Fashion footwear brochure.

DESIGN FIRM:

Cahan & Associates,

San Francisco, California

ART DIRECTOR: Bill Cahan

DESIGNER: David Gilmour

PHOTOGRAPHER:

David Peterson

QUANTITY: 1,000,000

PRINTING PROCESS: Web

Capabilities brochure.

DESIGN FIRM:

Axcess Group,

Atlanta, Georgia

ART DIRECTOR:

Bob Wages

DESIGNERS:

Raquel C. Miqueli,

Ted Fabella

COPYWRITER: Tony King

THERE MUST BE EQUAL OPPORTUNITY FOR EMPLOYMENT, DEVELOPMENT, AND ADVANCEMENT FOR THOSE QUALIFIED. WE MUST PROVIDE COMPETENT MANAGEMENT, AND ITS ACTIONS MUST BE JUST AND ETHICAL. ◐ WE ARE RESPONSIBLE TO THE COMMUNITIES IN WHICH WE LIVE AND WORK, AND TO THE WORLD COMMUNITY AS WELL. WE MUST BE GOOD CITIZENS, SUPPORT GOOD WORKS AND CHARITIES, AND BEAR OUR FAIR SHARE OF TAXES. WE MUST ENCOURAGE CIVIC IMPROVEMENTS AND BETTER HEALTH AND EDUCATION. WE MUST MAINTAIN, IN GOOD ORDER, THE PROPERTY WE ARE PRIVILEGED TO USE, PROTECTING THE ENVIRONMENT AND NATURAL RESOURCES. ◐ OUR FINAL RESPONSIBILITY IS TO OUR STOCKHOLDERS. BUSINESS MUST MAKE A SOUND PROFIT. WE MUST EXPERIMENT WITH NEW IDEAS. RESEARCH MUST BE CARRIED ON, INNOVATIVE PROGRAMS DEVELOPED, AND MISTAKES PAID FOR. NEW EQUIPMENT MUST BE PURCHASED, NEW FACILITIES PROVIDED, AND NEW PRODUCTS LAUNCHED. RESERVES MUST BE CREATED TO PROVIDE FOR ADVERSE TIMES. WHEN WE OPERATE ACCORDING TO THESE PRINCI-PLES, THE STOCKHOLDERS SHOULD REALIZE A FAIR RETURN.

Interface (Flooring)

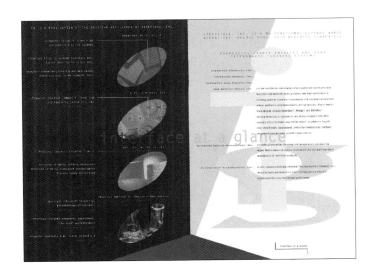

Promotion for Classic Crest line.

DESIGN FIRM:

Wages Design, Atlanta, Georgia

ART DIRECTOR:

Bob Wages

DESIGNER:

Raquel C. Miqueli

COPYWRITER:

Melissa James

PHOTOGRAPHERS:

Chris Callis, Parish Kohanim, Studio X, Mark Hanauer, Paul Elledge, Ann Cutting, John North Holtorf, Pete McArthur, Craig Cutler,

Marc Hauser, Elisabet Zeilon, John Clayton, Raquel C. Miqueli, Timothy White, David Sawyer, Laurie Rubin

ILLUSTRATOR:

Walt Floyd

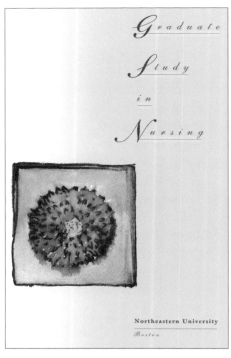

Graduate

Study

in

Nursing

Northeastern University

Boston

Community Health

Critical Care

The movement to provide health care where people live, work, and go to school is well underway. This shift to community-based health services has created challenging opportunities for community health nurses who manage every facet of home health care and hold leadership positions in the rapidly growing public health care system.

Northeastern's master's and certificate programs in community health emphasize the new epidemiological approach to health promotion and disease prevention for individuals, families, and communities. The concepts and techniques related to community assessment, organization, and empowerment are an integral part of the program. Courses specific to community health as well as to each of the two available concentrations are combined with professional nursing studies and electives. Opportunities to acquire the knowledge and skills of the nurse practitioner are available within this program.

In the critical care arena, nurses in advanced practice manage the complex care required by the most acutely ill patients and provide support to those in crisis. As an acute care practitioner, you will combine health promotion, restoration, and rehabilitation for patients across an entire episode of illness – from hospital to ambulatory clinic to home.

Sophisticated technology, nursing diagnosis, medical emergencies, and patient/family interventions come into play on a daily basis as do both crisis management and interpersonal skills. This is particularly evident in the Neonatal Nurse Practitioner concentration where working with the parents is every bit as important as providing expert care to the critically ill neonate.

Northeastern's master's and certificate programs combine courses specific to critical care and the two available concentrations with professional nursing studies and electives. You may choose electives that focus on pathophysiological assessment, technological monitoring, trauma, and immunosuppression. Opportunities to acquire the knowledge and skills of the nurse practitioner are integral to this program.

 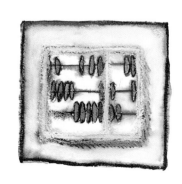

Prospectus.

DESIGN FIRM:

Geddis Productions,

Brookline, Massachusetts

ART DIRECTOR:

Pamela R. Geddis

DESIGNER: Diane Jaroch

ILLUSTRATOR:

Blair Thornley

QUANTITY: 10,000

PRINTING PROCESS:

Offset. Cover: 7/2 4-color

plus two PMS colors plus

off-line overall satin varnish

over two colors; text: 6/6

4-color plus one PMS color

plus PMS black; artwork:

12-color separations

Mobile, Alabama

Palo Alto, California   Santa Barbara, California

YELLOW CAB

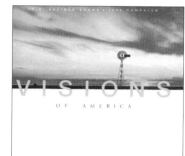

V I S I O N S

OF AMERICA

94

Questions and Answers

Promotion sent to members of 1994 Volunteer Committee for U.S. Savings Bonds.

DESIGN FIRM:

Belk-Mignogna Associates, Ltd., New York, New York

ART DIRECTOR:

Steve Mignogna

DESIGNERS:

Wendy Blattner,

Donna Dornbusch

PHOTOGRAPHERS:

Bob Day, Jim Karageorge,

Jeff Corwin

BUDGET: $150,000

QUANTITY: 32,000

PRINTING PROCESS:

Offset lithography

NYNEX Corporation (Telecommunications)

Promotional series for
special operations groups.

DESIGN FIRM:

Belk Mignogna Associates,
New York, New York

ART DIRECTOR:

Howard Belk

DESIGNER:

Victoria Stamm

BUDGET: $25,000 for
each brochure

QUANTITY: 10,000 of
each brochure

PRINTING PROCESS:

Offset lithography

Continental Corporations (Insurance)

Promotional book for the

artist's 1993 world tour.

DESIGN FIRM:

Design/Art, Inc,

Los Angeles, California

ART DIRECTOR/

DESIGNER: Norman Moore

PHOTOGRAPHER:

Albert Watson

QUANTITY: 50,000

PRINTING PROCESS:

Offset

sade love deluxe

RDM Management (Artist Management)

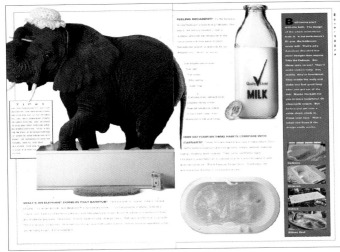

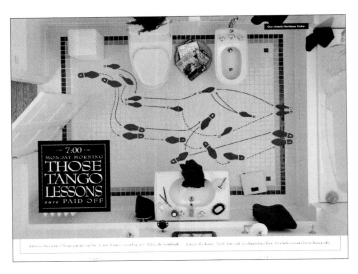

Promotional sales tool.

AGENCY:

Carmichael Lynch,

Minneapolis, Minnesota

ART DIRECTOR:

Peter Winecke

DESIGNER: Lars Hanson

ILLUSTRATOR:

Steve McHugh

COPYWRITER:

John Neumann

BUDGET: $365,000

QUANTITY: 350,000

PRINTING PROCESS:

6-color

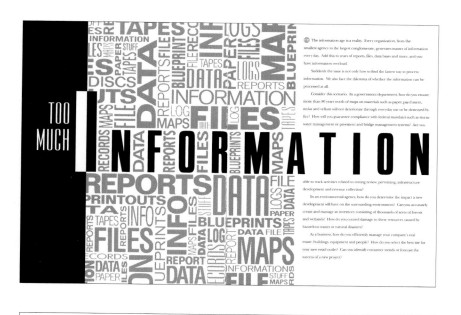

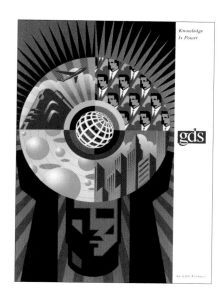

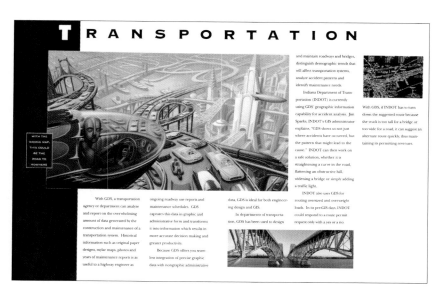

Promotion for Graphic
Data System software
program.

DESIGN FIRM:

Bartels & Company, Inc.,

St. Louis, Missouri

ART DIRECTOR:

David Bartels

DESIGNER: Brian Barclay

ILLUSTRATOR:

Bill Gantner

QUANTITY: 20,000

PRINTING PROCESS:

6-color lithography

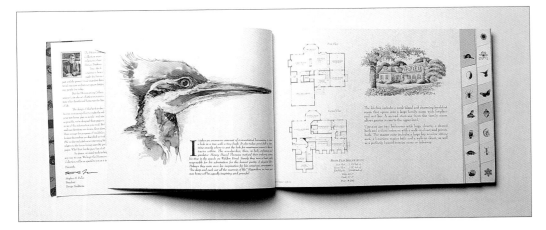

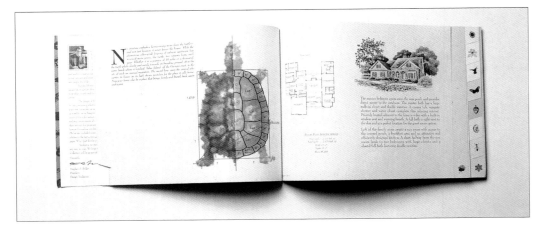

Sales booklet for a collection of home plans.

DESIGN FIRM:

Trousdell Design, Inc., Atlanta, Georgia

CREATIVE DIRECTOR:

Diana Thorington

ART DIRECTOR:

Don Trousdell

DESIGNER:

Brett Trousdell

ILLUSTRATOR:

Ted Burns (flower, woodpecker)

PRINTING PROCESS:

4-color with special black ink used to achieve richer effect on uncoated stock. Cover has two opaque inks for greater contrast on dark cover stock plus gold foil stamping.

Design Traditions (Home Design)

ESSE paper promotion.

DESIGN FIRM:

The Valentine Group,

New York, New York

ART DIRECTOR:

Robert Valentine

DESIGNERS:

Robert Valentine,

Wayne Wolf

ILLUSTRATOR:

Harry Bates,

Regan Dunnick

PHOTOGRAPHER:

Henny Garfunkel

COPYWRITER: Julie Iovine

PROJECT MANAGER:

Meg Stebbins

QUANTITY: 25,000

PRINTING PROCESS:

Offset lithography

BOXING IS PARADOX AS WELL AS SPORT. IT REPELS AS IT FASCINATES, ENGAGING THE LOFTIEST SENTIMENTS AT THE CRUDEST LEVEL. HARDLY POPULAR IN TERMS OF MASS ENTERTAINMENT, IT IS STILL THE MOST UNIVERSALLY APPEALING OF COMPETITIONS. ALTHOUGH UNATTRACTIVE TO MANY, BOXING PERTAINS TO THE HIGHEST DEGREE OF ELEMENTAL, EVEN INESCAPABLE TENDENCIES IN HUMANKIND: TOWARDS VIOLENCE EXPLOITATION, HEROISM, CONFRONTING MORTALITY.

KO

Gilbert Paper

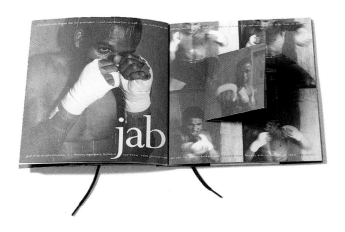

jab

blow by blow

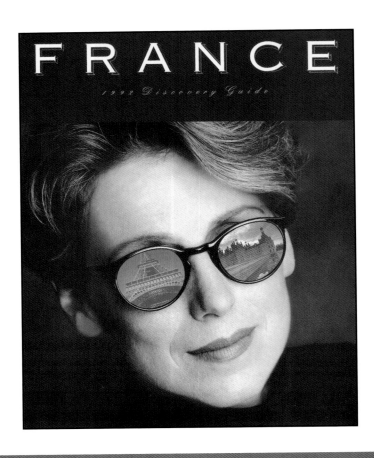

FRANCE
1992 Discovery Guide

Campaign designed to promote tourism in France.

DESIGN FIRM:

The Kuester Group, Minneapolis, Minnesota

ART DIRECTOR:

Kevin Kuester

DESIGNERS:

Brent Marmo, Bob Goebel, Tim Sauer

PHOTOGRAPHER:

Tom Berthiaume

QUANTITY: 500,000

PRINTING PROCESS:

4-color web

French Government Tourist Office

Cover (above, left) and spread (left) from tourist guide; cover (above, right) of Welcome Center directory; cover (below) of incentive coupon booklet sponsored by AT&T.

THERE
IS NO
DIFFERENCE
BETWEEN
NIGHT
AND DAY.

Direct-mail promotion for graduate school evening program.

DESIGN FIRM:

KSK Communications, Newton Highlands, Massachusetts

ART DIRECTOR/

DESIGNER: David Hadley

ILLUSTRATOR:

Douglas Smith

BUDGET: $2500

If you're serious enough to pursue your master's degree, you won't want to make any compromises in the quality of your education. That's why The George Washington University, unlike other master's programs, ensures the highest possible calibre of instruction to all of our part-time students. They study with the same distinguished faculty as those who are enrolled full-time. You will also have access to the resources, study group discussions, and overall academic experience that our full-time students enjoy. And once you graduate, you'll find that your professors will still be available to advise you, write letters of reference, and otherwise assist you in making important career contacts.

CREDENTIALS
FOR THE REAL WORLD
We realize that the qualifications you need to reach the top of your profession are in constant flux. That's why all our programs are designed to keep pace with these changing requirements. One way in which we meet

OUR NIGHT STUDENTS STUDY WITH THE SAME OUTSTANDING PROFESSORS AS OUR DAY STUDENTS

this challenge is by successfully balancing the theoretical and the practical aspects of each of our master's programs.

Our faculty has earned a reputation for the invaluable first-hand knowledge they impart to their students. For instance, at the Elliott School of International Affairs, you'll study with former presidential advisers and senior diplomats. Our internationally recognized School of Medicine and Health Sciences puts you in touch with professors who have played a pivotal role in drafting crucial health care legislation. You'll benefit from our connections to national and international business interests as well as the strong global perspective at the School of Business and Public Management. In our School of Engineering and Applied Sciences, you will study with faculty who have earned international recog-

nition for significant contributions to their field.

Because certain fields of study call for overlapping expertise, we frequently incorporate courses from multiple disciplines to form cohesive, in-depth programs that address current social, economic, technical, and political issues. The George Washington University's National Law Center offers a number of special programs in which you may earn joint degrees with other George Washington University graduate schools.

CONVENIENCE AS WELL
AS EXCELLENCE
Aside from our worldwide

reputation for the highest academic standards, we are also easy to reach at our convenient locations in the District of Columbia and northern Virginia. Our Foggy Bottom Campus (just five blocks from the White House) is close to the Metro. And we have class schedules flexible enough to meet the needs of part-time students.

A WIDER SELECTION
OF PROGRAMS
THAN YOU'LL FIND
ANYWHERE
We offer the most comprehensive range of programs in the Washington area, with over 170 master's degrees and more than 60 doctoral degree programs.

For more information, please call us at (202) 994-3900.

The George Washington University
WASHINGTON DC

Master's Programs
CREDENTIALS FOR THE REAL WORLD

The George Washington University's policies provide for equal opportunity in employment and admission to all programs of the University.

George Washington University

Catalog of historic and
original stock illustrations.

DESIGN FIRM:

Charles S. Anderson
Design Company,
Minneapolis, Minnesota

ART DIRECTOR:

Charles S. Anderson

DESIGNERS:

Charles S. Anderson,

Todd Piper-Hauswirth

COPYWRITER:

Lisa Pemrick

IP MEAD ESCANABA ENAMEL MEAD S
E DULL WEB MEAD MOISTRITE MAT
ULL MEAD NORTHCOTE FREE MEAD N
EAD SIGNATURE GLOSS WEB MEAD S
TE MATTE WEB MEAD WEB ENAMEL M
MEAD NORTHCOTE RMP MEAD ESCA
S WEB MEAD SIGNATURE DULL WEB
EB ENAMEL ME **MEAD** DULL MEAD N
IP MEAD ESCA ENAMEL MEAD
URE DULL WEB MEAD MOISTRITE MA
MEAD NORTHCOTE FREE MEAD NOR
L MEAD SIGNATURE GLOSS WEB MEA
TE MATTE WEB MEAD WEB ENAMEL M
MEAD NORTHCOTE RMP MEAD ESCAN
SS WEB MEAD SIGNATURE DULL WE
EB ENAMEL MEAD WEB DULL MEAD N
IP MEAD ESCANABA ENAMEL MEAD S

Envelope.

Paper promotion series.

DESIGN FIRM:

Van Dyke Company,

Seattle, Washington

ART DIRECTOR:

John Van Dyke

DESIGNERS:

John Van Dyke,

Ann Kumasaka

PHOTOGRAPHERS:

Richard Berenholtz

(Northcote RMP);

Jim Sims, Rick Rusing

(Signature Gloss);

Kathryn Kleinman

(Moistrite Matte)

COPYWRITER: Jon Bell

QUANTITY: 20,000 each

PRINTING PROCESS:

2/4 black plus PMS/

4-color other side; web.

Mead Northcote® RMP.
Words to the wise:
Catalog your savings.
Give weighty matters a
light touch. Post smal-
ler bills. This paper is
a postage beater. Nice
and light. Penny-wise.
Pound-wise. Wise choice.

Mead Signature® Gloss Web. Image is one thing, fashion is another. And the paper you put the image on is a fashion statement. Because in the real world, where ink hits the paper, appearance is reality.

Mead Moistrite® Matte Web. To create any-thing truly new, inno-vators begin where the most current technol-ogy ends. Only then can they lean over the edge to yank the previously unthinkable into being.

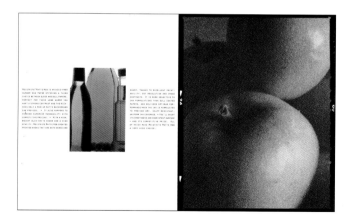

'etaoin shrdlu'

Graduate design student project.

DESIGN FIRM: University of Illinois at Urbana-Champaign, Art & Design, Graphic Design, Champaign, Illinois

ART DIRECTOR: Nan Goggin

DESIGNERS: Fred Daab, Brian Curray, Gregg Synder, Nan Goggin, Mark Fetkewicz, Elizabeth A. Postmus, Paula Curran, Christina Nordholm, Karen Cole, Jeff Clift, Fanky Chak, Vince Parker, Joe Kukella, Chris Waegner

PRINTER: Office of Printing Services, University of Illinois at Urbana-Champaign

QUANTITY: 150

PRINTING PROCESS: Hand printed on Vandercook proofing press, hand set metal type

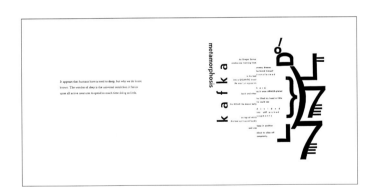

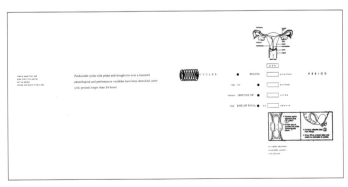

Karma paper promotion.

DESIGN FIRM:

The Kuester Group,

Minneapolis, Minnesota

ART DIRECTOR:

Kevin B. Kuester

DESIGNERS: Bill Thorburn,

Kevin B. Kuester

ILLUSTRATOR: J.A. Molly

PHOTOGRAPHER:

Don Freeman

COPYWRITER:

David Forney

QUANTITY: 50,000

PRINTING PROCESS:

4-color with in-line metallics

Potlatch Corporation (Paper Manufacturer)

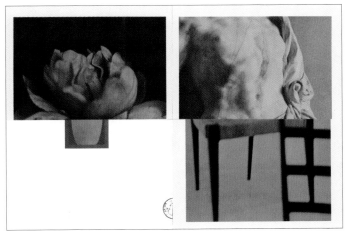

Self-promotion for
marketing/image
consultants.
ART DIRECTOR:
Barry Shepard/SHR
Perceptual Management,
Scottsdale, Arizona
DESIGNERS: Mike Shanks,
Nathan Joseph
PRODUCTION:
Roger Barger
PHOTOGRAPHER:
Rodney Rascona
QUANTITY: 2000
PRINTING PROCESS:
Sheet-fed

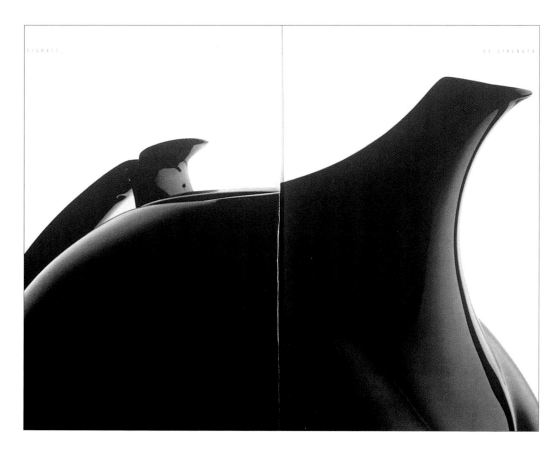

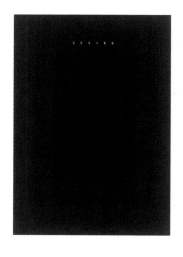

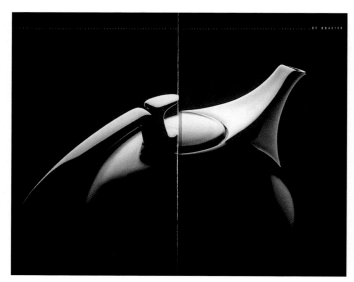

SHR Perceptual Management

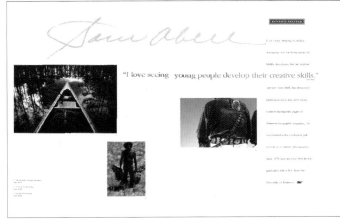

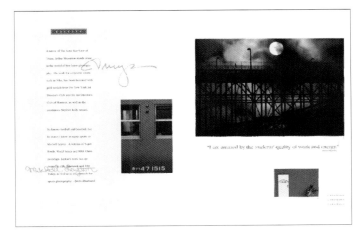

Promotion/application for National Photography Institute/Hot Shots program offered by the National 4-H Council.

DESIGN FIRM: Cornerstone, Baltimore, Maryland

ART DIRECTOR/ DESIGNER: Jennifer Milne

COPYWRITER: Jack Gilden

PRINTER: Indiana Press, Inc.

PRINTING PROCESS: 4-color

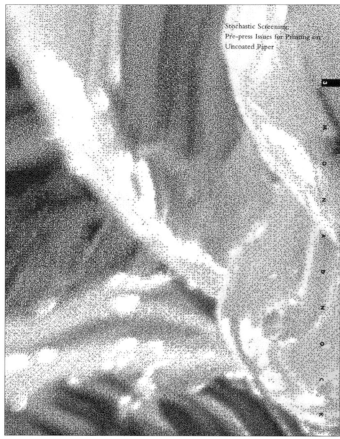

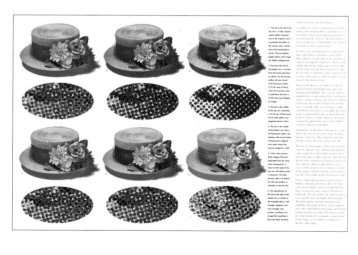

Paper promotion series.

DESIGN FIRM:

Chermayeff & Geismar,

New York, New York

ART DIRECTOR:

Tom Geismar

DESIGNER: Cathy Schaefer

PHOTOGRAPHER:

David Arky

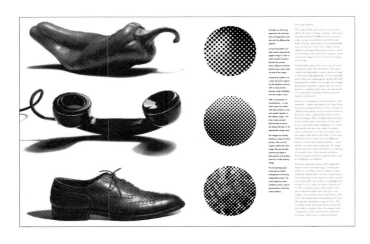

Consumer information
booklet that explains
menopause and the
benefits/risks of estrogen
replacement therapy.
DESIGN FIRM:
Grafik Communications Ltd.,
Alexandria, Virginia
DESIGNERS: Melanie Bass,
Judy F. Kirpich
ILLUSTRATOR:
Melanie Bass
COPYWRITER:
Leslie Waldman
QUANTITY: 5000
PRINTING PROCESS:
Standard offset

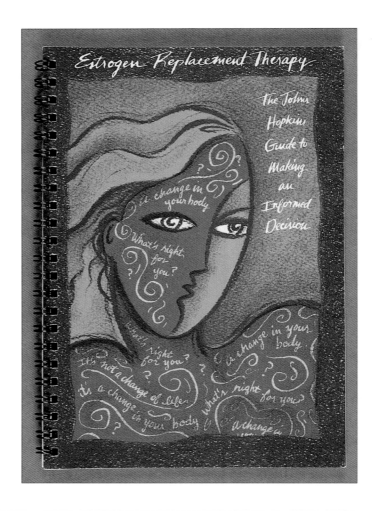

Johns Hopkins University

What about Changes in the Urethra, Bladder and Vagina? Estrogen has a significant influence on cells that make up the lining of the urethra and vagina. When estrogen decreases in menopause, there is a corresponding drop in the number of cells lining the vagina; its natural lubrication diminishes, and its lining becomes thin and easily injured — and having sex may become painful. A drop in estrogen also may thin the cells lining the urethra — which are important in preventing urine from leaking. This may increase the chance of urinary incontinence, as a thinner lining lowers the pressure inside the urethra, and allows the urine to escape more easily. ERT may help ease some of these symptoms.

What about Psychological Changes? One psychological problem often attributed to menopause is depression. However, the frequency of depression increases as we get older. So does menopause cause an increase in mental health problems? This question remains unresolved. ☉ What is clear is that **it's too simplistic to blame any change in a woman's mental status only on menopause.** Other factors may be responsible, and a complete workup may be needed to diagnose and treat the underlying problem.

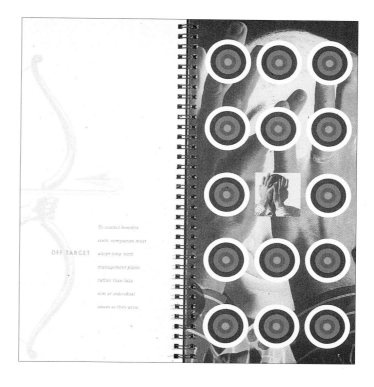

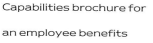

Capabilities brochure for an employee benefits management consultant.

DESIGN FIRM:

WYD Design, Inc.,

Westport, Connecticut

ART DIRECTOR/

COPYWRITER:

Frank Oswald

DESIGNER:

Scott Kuykendall

PHOTOGRAPHER:

Geoffrey Stein

PRODUCTION

MANAGER: Suzie Yannes

QUANTITY: 2500

PRINTING PROCESS:

Screen process, blind embossed, cover tipped in, 4-color plus spot colors

Corporate Health Strategies

Promotional compilation of work produced during a workshop in which participants spent 18 hours photographing their environment.

DESIGN FIRM:

University and College Designers Association, Glen Ellyn, Illinois

ART DIRECTORS:

Jody Zamirowski, Jean Springer, Chris Klonowski

DESIGNER:

Julius Friedman

PHOTOGRAPHERS:

Julius Friedman (top), Mark Brady (center, left), Jody Zamirowski (center, right), Connie Peterson (bottom)

BUDGET: Supplier donations

QUANTITY: 30,000

PRINTING PROCESS: 4-color offset

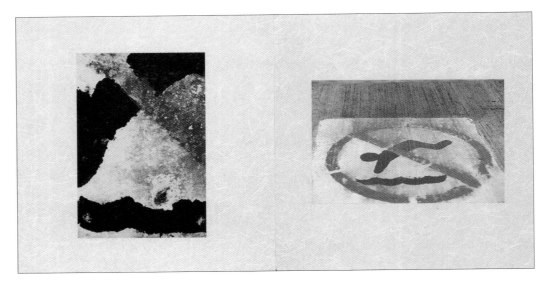

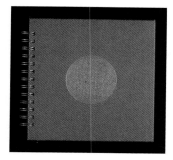

Capabilities brochure for

a brokered reinsurance

firm.

DESIGN FIRM:

WYD Design, Inc.,

Westport, Connecticut

ART DIRECTOR:

Frank J. Oswald

DESIGNERS:

Scott Kuykendall,

David Dunkelberger

PRODUCTION MANAGER:

Suzie Yannes

QUANTITY: 5000

PRINTING PROCESS:

Blind-embossed, foil-

stamped, 4-color plus

spot colors

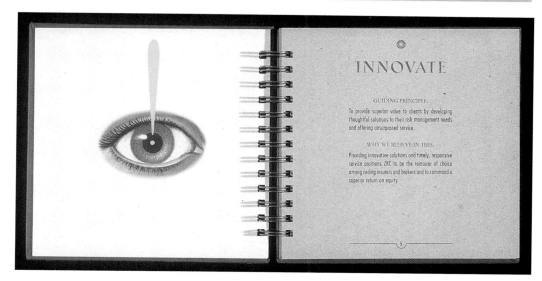

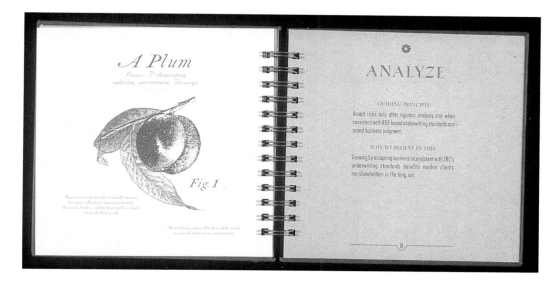

FOR THE LAST 25 YEARS, the legal profession has been experimenting to learn whether requiring lawyers to follow detailed rules would improve professional conduct. I describe the effort as an experiment, because we so quickly forget that rule-oriented legal ethics is really a recent development. ■ Most of today's graduates were born before 1969, the year the ABA published its first Model Code of Professional Responsibility. That code was widely adopted by the states, but it proved so problematic that by 1983, when

Going Beyond Ethical Codes

most of you were at least in high school, the ABA had adopted a new set of standards, the Model Rules of Professional Conduct. ■ At least two-thirds of lawyers now in practice received their ethics training under these sets of standards, so we tend to think they have governed us forever. A century ago, however, only Alabama had codified even general requirements for lawyer behavior, the "canons" of lawyer ethics. It was not until 1908 that the ABA proposed such "Canons of Ethics" for wider use.

Thomas D. Morgan

This address was given at the J. Reuben Clark Law School Convocation Exercises, April 24, 1992.

ILLUSTRATIONS BY PATRICIA LANGUEDOC

Law school publication.

ILLUSTRATOR:

Patricia Languedoc,

Santa Barbara, California

ART DIRECTOR/

DESIGNER: Linda Sullivan

A CAMELOT FOR SCOTT

CRYPTOGRAPHERS

Minet specialists know their clients' businesses and can decipher the most complex industry-specific risks and challenges.

In today's world, there are few straightforward risks or opportunities. Most are twisted, raveled and furled. They speak many languages, and hide within the convolutions of different industries and professions.

Minet extricates clients from this information jungle. We scrutinize the inscrutable and clarify contradictions that often confound traditionalists. Like skilled cryptographers, our specialists work assiduously to break through surface issues to reach the heart of each company's real needs.

Our brokers are recognised as leaders in their fields and the insurance industry. Many were risk managers, senior executives and advisors in the industries we serve, providing them with first-hand, in-depth knowledge to decipher complex risks and liabilities.

To complement these individuals, we employ a diverse staff of professionals with backgrounds in finance, law, engineering, statistics and other disciplines to consult with clients and provide fresh perspectives on significant business challenges.

This creative, multi-disciplinary approach to problem solving enables us to provide a more thorough and accurate analysis of our clients' risk management needs and a level of service that we believe is unique within the broker industry.

Open and Shut Case

A restraining order against the assets of a major U.S. law firm threatened its ability to operate. Partners had to resolve a maze of complex issues by a Monday deadline or the firm's doors would be closed. Leveraging strong market relationships, Minet rallied lead underwriters on two continents and negotiated an around-the-clock weekend settlement to avert the conflict.

Minet is led by innovators and synergists—specialists with foresight to do more than respond to today's needs; they anticipate future challenges and help clients master change within some of the most demanding industries and professions in the world.

FUTURISTS

Minet is at the forefront of change in the insurance industry and an augur of emerging business conditions and trends.

Throughout our history, Minet has been a prime mover in developing new risk management concepts. Notably, we pioneered professional liability coverage more than 50 years ago and continue to lead the market in developing new innovations to protect professional service firms and the directors and officers of leading corporations and financial institutions.

Minet works vigorously to open new frontiers of opportunity for clients through the collaborative development of new products and services within our organisation. These creative efforts have often led to meaningful, new risk management solutions, including unique coverages to protect enterprises from emerging liabilities.

Long before 'globalisation' and 'specialization' became industry buzz words, they were disciplines at Minet. We will continue this progressive approach to business to keep our clients a step ahead in their respective industries.

A League of Their Own

Minet foresaw the turmoil that would engulf the professional liability market in the 1980s. To protect the accounting industry from the resulting exposures, we assisted the major international firms in setting aside competitive differences and forming a cooperative risk-sharing venture. The result is one of the most creative and substantial captive insurers in the world.

Minet Group

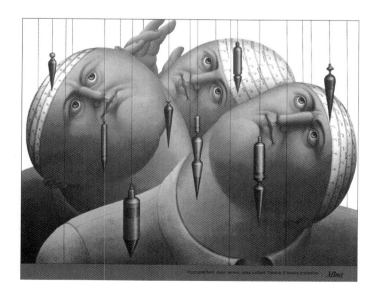

Cryptographers, shed names, wrap surfaces Scholte & blazek protection   *Minet*

Capabilities brochure for a risk management insurance broker.

DESIGN FIRM: WYD Design, Inc., Westport, Connecticut

ART DIRECTOR/ COPYWRITER: Frank J. Oswald

DESIGNERS: Scott Kuykendall,

Frank J. Oswald

ILLUSTRATORS: Roy Carruthers, John Kleber

PRODUCTION MANAGER: Suzie Yannes

QUANTITY: 25,000

PRINTING PROCESS: 4-color plus four spot colors

Paper promotion for

Reflections paper line

that was originally a self-

promotion for

photographer Les

Jörgensen.

ART DIRECTOR/

DESIGNER:

Roland Dahlquist,

New York, New York

ILLUSTRATOR/

PHOTOGRAPHER:

Les Jörgensen

COPYWRITER:

Sara Harrell

QUANTITY: 35,000

PRINTING PROCESS:

4-color lithography plus

gloss varnish

Consolidated Papers, Inc.

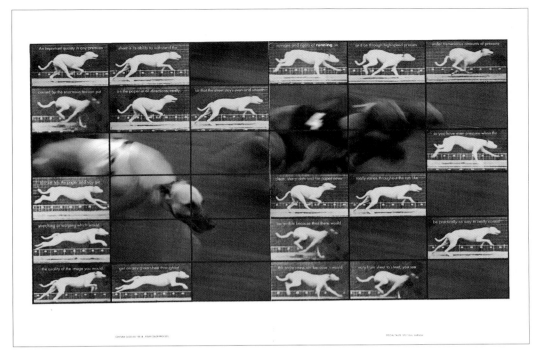

Paper promotion.

DESIGN FIRM:

Petrick Design,

Chicago, Illinois

ART DIRECTOR:

Robert Petrick

DESIGNERS:

Robert Petrick, Tim Fisher

QUANTITY: 25,000

PRINTING PROCESS:

1 pass through a 6-color

press

When **folding** coated paper, it should be scored to avoid cracking, especially if it is laid out against the grain or the fold runs through an area of heavy ink coverage. Any job with a gatefold should be scored at the thumb edge to help prevent cracking and to make the job lie flatter. Cover stock should always be scored, no matter what the grain direction. For best results in scoring, a letter-press channel score should be used.

Consolidated Papers, Inc.

Promotional brochure.

DESIGN FIRM:

Grafik Communications Ltd.,

Alexandria, Virginia

ART DIRECTORS:

Jim Jackson, Judy Kirpich

PHOTOGRAPHER:

Walter Bigbee

PRINTING PROCESS:

Offset

National Museum of the American Indian

Promotion for artists'
representative.
DESIGN FIRM:
Haley Johnson Design
Company,
Minneapolis, Minnesota
DESIGNER: Haley Johnson

Photo by George Peer

PHILIP B. CROSBY IS ONE OF AMERICA'S LEADING QUALITY EXPERTS. HIS LESSONS AND APPROACH HAVE BECOME A CORNERSTONE OF THE BELL ATLANTIC QUALITY TRAINING INSTITUTE. TO ILLUSTRATE THE NEED FOR A 100% DEDICATION TO QUALITY HE RETELLS CHARLES DICKENS' "A CHRISTMAS CAROL" WITH A QUALITY TWIST. THE MAIN CHARACTER IS VISITED BY THE GHOST OF HIS LONG-DEAD BUSINESS PARTNER. THE BUSINESS PARTNER LANGUISHES IN A DISMAL AFTERLIFE DESTINED TO CORRECT THE QUALITY FAILURES HE MADE WHILE LIVING. HE SPENDS HIS AFTERLIFE REPAIRING LEAKING WASHING MACHINES, FLAMING TOASTERS, AND BAD IRON CASTINGS. AND NEXT TO THIS GHOSTLY PARTNER IS AN OFFICE FULL OF FAULTY PRODUCTS WAITING FOR OUR HERO. NEEDLESS TO SAY, THE HERO SEES THE ERROR OF HIS WAYS. IT'S A STORY WITH A HUMOROUS TONE, BUT ITS MESSAGE IS ANYTHING BUT FUNNY. IN THE STORY, AS IT IS IN LIFE, DEFECTS RETURN TO HAUNT THOSE WHO CREATE THEM. SO AT BELL ATLANTIC, WE CONCENTRATE ON DOING OUR JOBS RIGHT THE FIRST TIME, EVERY TIME.

Bell Atlantic

Employee recruitment brochure.
AGENCY:
Holmes & Associates,
Los Angeles, California
ART DIRECTOR/
DESIGNER:
Michele Holmes
ILLUSTRATOR:
Joel Nakamura
COPYWRITER:
Mitchell Obatake
PRINTER: Cardinal Printing

QUANTITY: 10,000
PRINTING PROCESS:
Lithography

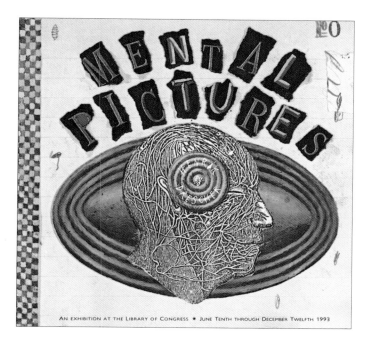

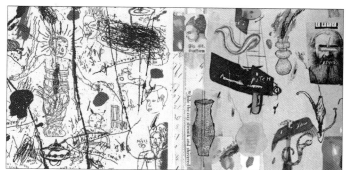

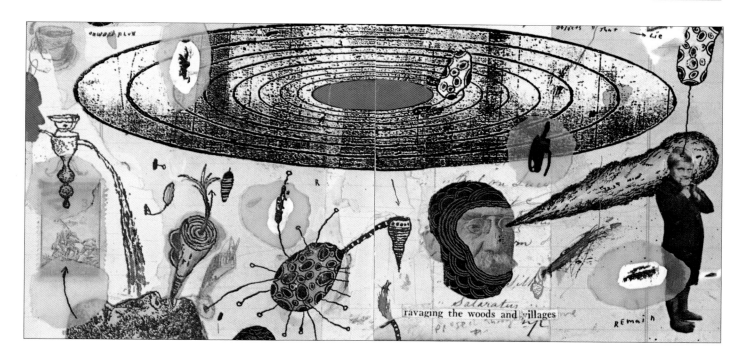

Henrik Drescher

exhibition brochure.

DESIGN FIRM:

Grafik Communications Ltd.,

Alexandria, Virginia

DESIGNERS:

Judy F. Kirpich,

Julie Sebastianelli

ILLUSTRATOR:

Henrik Drescher

PRINTING PROCESS:

Standard offset

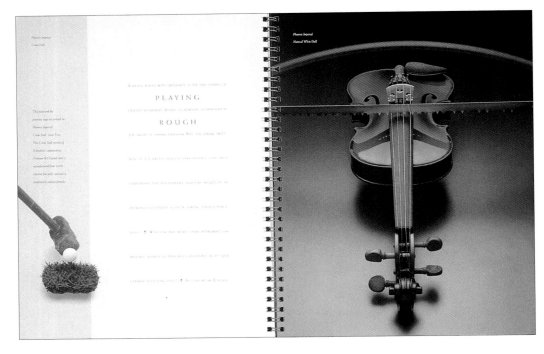

Promotion targeting U.S. designers.

DESIGN FIRM:

Brian J. Ganton &

Associates,

Cedar Grove, New Jersey

ART DIRECTOR:

Brian J. Ganton Jr.

DESIGNERS:

Brian J. Ganton Jr.,

Mark Ganton

PHOTOGRAPHER:

Christopher Ganton

COPYWRITER:

Brian J. Ganton Sr.

QUANTITY: 10,000

PRINTING PROCESS:

Offset lithography

WE'RE INVESTING UP TO $10 MILLION ON PLANT UPGRADES TO OUR DEDICATED PLANT. AND THAT'S ONLY THE START.

While the regulatory environment demands more from your product, we're responding with more for your product. And it targets with a substantial investment in capital improvements.

Our dedicated manufacturing plant already operates under GMP and ISO 9002 standards. But we know this is no time to rest on our laurels. World-class manufacturing status is a moving target that requires a continued dedication to improvement.

This means Dow Corning will be spending as much as $9 million in the next two years to assure our manufacturing keeps pace with new regulatory demands and the demands of a global market. We'll be examining all our processes from top to bottom to reduce cost, time, and waste, and to improve our capabilities. And we'll be spending up to $1 million on testing our Medical Grade material to meet selected tests for Tripartite guidelines and ISO standards. The result? Better products for world-class performance. And a competitive advantage passed on to our customers.

To support these capital investments, we are also investing 20-25 effort years from a corporation-wide team of experts drawn from manufacturing, production, testing and technical service. Together with our operational staff they will ensure that our plant delivers optimal performance to meet your most demanding standards.

Our aim is not simply to provide you with the performance you require, but with the leadership and quality you expect. At Dow Corning, you can count on a resolve to create and maintain a manufacturing resource of the highest order. We will continue to offer capabilities above and beyond the call of "business as usual" like our technical service and research team offering a combined total of more than 150 years of experience.

Upgraded, dedicated manufacturing, supported by personnel and a concentration on Medical Grade products: these are the means we focus on your business, for your success. To discuss further how your applications can benefit from our world-class manufacturing and our expanded capabilities, contact Ginger Hall, Quality Assurance Manager of our Hemlock plant, 1-800-833-9008, ext. 103.

Dow Corning Medical

Medical materials brochure directed to the healthcare industry.

AGENCY: Aves, Inc., Grand Rapids, Michigan

ART DIRECTOR/ DESIGNER: Jim Markle

ILLUSTRATORS: Marianna Hughes (cover), Kent Barton (shown, top right), Rose Rosely (shown, top right), David Chen, Bob Werner and Roy Tahtinen (shown, bottom right), Gary Eldridge, Walt Deray (spot illustration)

COPYWRITER: Bill Harris

QUANTITY: 3500

PRINTING PROCESS: 4-color offset

The best material is always the one that fits the customer.

As more novel approaches are explored within drug delivery, the challenges facing designers and formulators have become more acute. The lack of specifically designed component materials only increases the difficulty of developing effective drug delivery systems. Expecting suppliers to have available all their material requirements on the shelf, in commercial quantities, and ready to use is highly desirable but not always possible.

So at Dow Corning we have committed ourselves to developing specific, customer-focused business relationships. These relationships allow you to gain maximum advantage from optimized products for your specific requirements. We work together, side by side, on projects of mutual benefit.

These are defined relationships, focused on the specific needs of the customer's project. The relationship is exclusive and confidential. We put it in writing.

These relationships form the context in which our technical capacity can be unleashed. The possibilities are wide open, as you may know from our innovations in transdermal technology. That work continues. We are also aggressively exploring new applications, new products, and other forms of drug delivery.

We offer access to one of the best chemistry sets around — our silicone technologies. And we have the supporting expertise to put it to work. You'll find it useful in oral sustained release, muco-adhesives, and transdermal systems to name a few.

Our technological capacity extends across a global network to the advantage of our customers. The results of successful collaborations can be seen in the numerous products worldwide incorporating Dow Corning formulations and technology.

Whether your need is for applied silicone technologies or silicone products, you can be sure that we are in this business for your long-term success. To further explore the advantages of a collaborative relationship, or to learn more about Dow Corning silicones for pharmaceutical applications call John Winland at 1-800-833-9008, ext. 105.

Paper promotion.

DESIGN FIRM:

Pentagram Design,

San Francisco, California

ART DIRECTOR:

Kit Hinrichs

DESIGNER: Belle How

PHOTOGRAPHER:

Bob Esparza

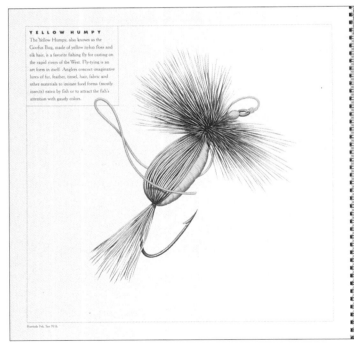

YELLOW HUMPY
The Yellow Humpy, also known as the Goofus Bug, made of yellow nylon floss and elk hair, is a favorite fishing fly for casting on the rapid rivers of the West. Fly-tying is an art form in itself. Anglers concoct imaginative lures of fur, feather, tinsel, hair, fabric and other materials to imitate food forms (mostly insects) eaten by fish or to attract the fish's attention with gaudy colors.

ZUNI FETISH
Zuni Indians keep small stone carvings of animal figures as fetishes, which represent spirits that have taken on the form of animals. Originally used in hunting ceremonies as a source of good luck, these replicas have kept their charm over the years, appealing to people of different cultures and backgrounds.
Often seen as jewelry, Zuni fetishes act as a symbol of peace and harmony with the spiritual world.

Paper promotions.

DESIGN FIRM:

Weymouth Design,

Bennington,

New Hampshire

ART DIRECTOR:

Michael Weymouth

PRODUCTION:

Daniels Printing

PHOTOGRAPHERS:

Susan Segal, George

Petrakes, Jeffery

Titcomb, Bruce Rogovin,

Sanjay Kothari, Michael

Weymouth

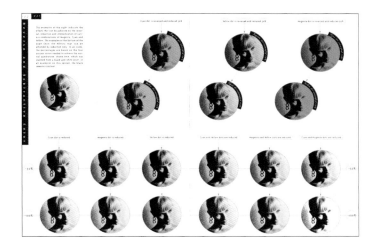

NEOTONE

3

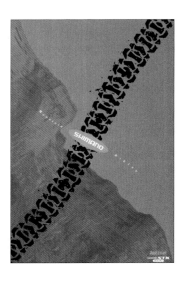

Shimano Bicycling (Bicycle Components)

Direct mail/point-of-purchase promotion targeting two markets—cycling enthusiasts and novice recreational riders.

DESIGN FIRM:

dGWB Advertising, Irvine, California

ART DIRECTOR:

Wade Koniakowsky

DESIGNER:

Sakol Mongol Kasetarin

COPYWRITER:

Hallie Pfieffer

ILLUSTRATOR:

Kevin Short

PHOTOGRAPHERS:

Kevin Reimers, Tom Hollar

BUDGET: $60,000

QUANTITY: 75,000

PRINTING PROCESS:

4-color offset

Series of print ads in the same promotional campaign.

1993–94 catalog for an outerwear manufacturer for the U.S. military.

AGENCY:

Siquis, Ltd./Baltimore, Annapolis, Maryland

ART DIRECTOR:

Rosemary Conroy

DESIGNER: Joe Barsin

PHOTOGRAPHER:

Charles Freeman

COPYWRITER:

Tom Daniels

BUDGET: $157,000

QUANTITY: 30,000

PRINTING PROCESS:

Sheet-fed, offset lithography

Direct-mail catalog for a marketer of specialty food products.

AGENCY:

Sarah Fisher Marketing, Cincinnati, Ohio

ART DIRECTOR/

DESIGNER/ILLUSTRATOR/

COPYWRITER:

Sarah Fisher

BUDGET: $25,000

QUANTITY: 50,000

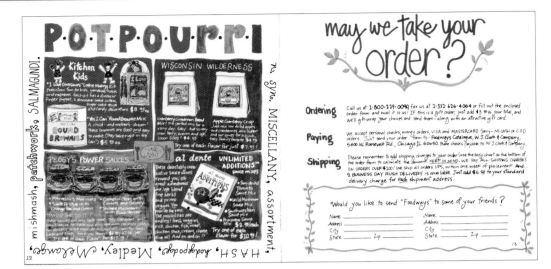

Above: envelope for catalog;
right: catalog cover.

Paper promotion

DESIGN FIRM:

The Kuester Group,

Minneapolis, Minnesota

ART DIRECTOR:

Kevin B. Kuester

DESIGNER: Tim Sauer

COPYWRITER:

David Forney

QUANTITY: 60,000

PRINTING PROCESS:

4-color

Simpson Paper Company

Paper promotion.

DESIGN FIRM:

Pentagram Design,

New York, New York

ART DIRECTOR:

Woody Pirtle

DESIGNERS: Woody Pirtle,

John Klotnia, Ron Louie,

Ivette Montes de Oca

COPYWRITERS:

Arnold & Underwood

PRINTER: Heritage Press

QUANTITY: 60,000

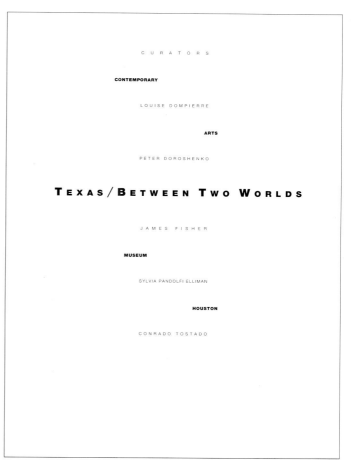

CURATORS

CONTEMPORARY

LOUISE DOMPIERRE

ARTS

PETER DOROSHENKO

TEXAS/BETWEEN TWO WORLDS

JAMES FISHER

MUSEUM

SYLVIA PANDOLFI ELLIMAN

HOUSTON

CONRADO TOSTADO

Contemporary Arts Museum, Houston

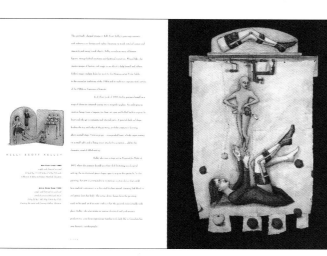

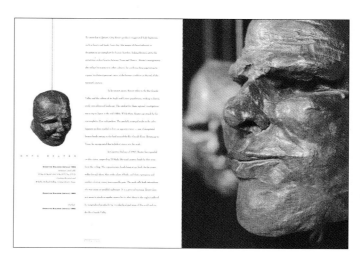

Catalog for an exhibition of contemporary Texas artists.

DESIGN FIRM:

Rigsby Design, Inc., Houston, Texas

ART DIRECTOR:

Lana Rigsby

DESIGNERS:

Lana Rigsby, Troy S. Ford

COVER PHOTOGRAPHERS:

Chris Shinn, Lynn Girouard

COPYWRITER:

Peter Doroshenko

QUANTITY: 1500

PRINTING PROCESS:

Sheet-fed

Promotion for Decade 10
paper line.
DESIGN FIRM:
The Kuester Group,
Minneapolis, Minnesota
ART DIRECTOR:
Kevin B. Kuester
DESIGNER: Bob Goebel
COPYWRITER:
David Forney
QUANTITY: 50,000
PRINTING PROCESS:
4-color

Potlatch Corporation (Paper Manufacturer)

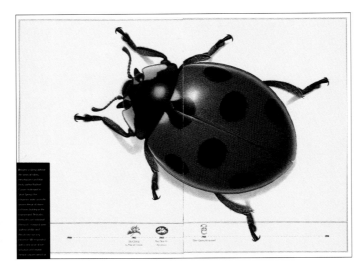

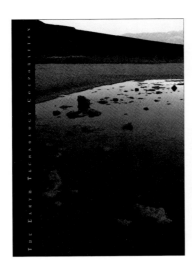

The Earth Technology Corporation

Capabilities brochure for a provider of environmental, earth sciences and waste management consulting services.

DESIGN FIRM:

Rigsby Design, Inc.,

Houston, Texas

ART DIRECTOR:

Lana Rigsby

DESIGNERS:

Lana Rigsby, Troy S. Ford

PRINCIPAL

PHOTOGRAPHERS:

Gary Faye,

Arthur Meyerson

COPYWRITER:

JoAnn Stone

QUANTITY: 7500

PRINTING PROCESS:

Sheet-fed

Promotion for a sound

recordings archive.

DESIGN FIRM:

Pentagram Design,

San Francisco, California

ART DIRECTOR:

Kit Hinrichs

DESIGNER: Jackie Foshaug

PHOTOGRAPHER:

Flip Hicklin

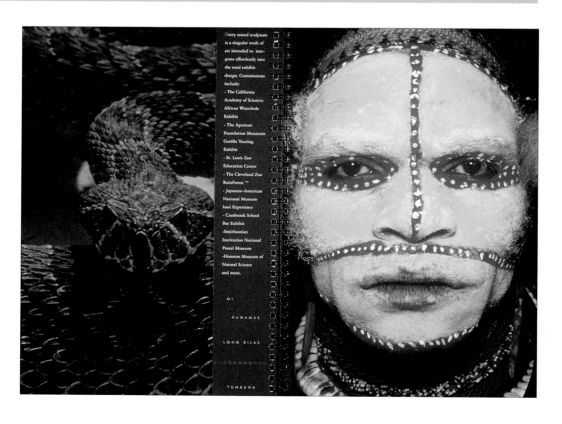

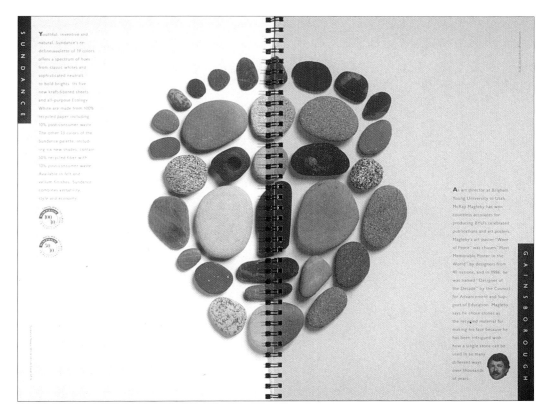

Simpson Paper Company

Promotion for recycled

papers.

DESIGN FIRM:

Pentagram Design,

San Francisco, California

ART DIRECTOR:

Kit Hinrichs

DESIGNERS: Belle How,

Amy Chan

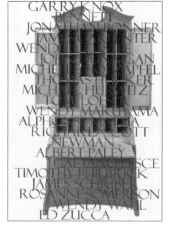

Catalog for the second group show of all the gallery's artists.

DESIGN FIRM: Pentagram Design, New York, New York

ART DIRECTOR: Michael Bierut

DESIGNER: Esther Bridavsky

BUDGET: $7500

QUANTITY: 7000

PRINTING PROCESS: Dry-trap printing

Promotion targeting food retailers.

DESIGN FIRM:

Bailey Lauerman & Associates,

Lincoln, Nebraska

ART DIRECTOR/ DESIGNER: Ron Sack

PHOTOGRAPHER:

Bob Ervin

COPYWRITER:

Mitch Koch

FOOD STYLIST:

Carrie Rennie

BUDGET: $18,000

QUANTITY: 2500

PRINTING PROCESS:

Offset, 5-color plus varnish

LaRosa Pasta Company (Pasta Manufacturer)

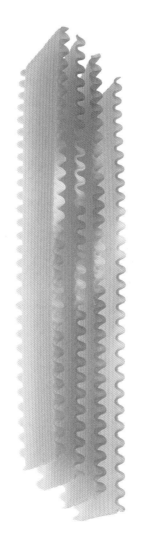

Today, this business that was founded in the back of a small grocery store is a wholly owned subsidiary of Archer-Daniels-Midland Company (ADM). And we're growing faster and in more directions than ever before. ¶ Thanks to our association with ADM, the largest agri-business corporation in the world, we now have two manu-

LaRosa the company.

facturing sites—one in Steger, Illinois, and another in Lincoln, Nebraska. Having two locations helps us handle big orders on a timely basis. Serving large regions is easier with two plants, as well. It's allowed us to be successful in markets everywhere from Michigan to Puerto Rico. ¶ LaRosa has even been able to expand beyond retail into the rapidly growing private label, industrial, and

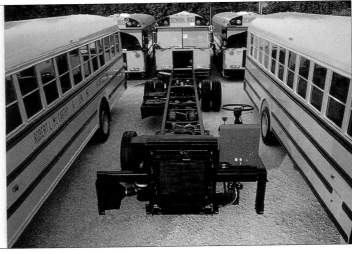

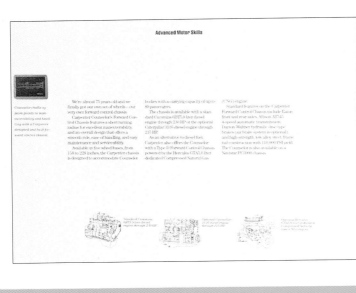

Advanced Motor Skills

We're almost 75 years old and we finally got our own set of wheels—our very own forward control chassis.

Carpenter Counselor's Forward Control Chassis features a short turning radius for excellent maneuverability and an overall design that offers a smooth ride, ease of handling, and easy maintenance and serviceability.

Available in five wheel bases, from 158 to 228 inches, the Carpenter chassis is designed to accommodate Counselor bodies with a carrying capacity of up to 80 passengers.

The chassis is available with a standard Cummins 6BT5.9 liter diesel engine through 230 HP or the optional Caterpillar 3116 diesel engine through 215 HP.

As an alternative to diesel fuel, Carpenter also offers the Counselor with a Type D Forward Control Chassis powered by the Hercules GTA5.6 liter dedicated Compressed Natural Gas (CNG) engine.

Standard features on the Carpenter Forward Control Chassis include Eaton front and rear axles, Allison AT545 4-speed automatic transmission, Dayton Walther hydraulic disc type brakes (air brake system is optional), and high strength, low alloy steel frame rail construction with 110,000 PSI yield. The Counselor is also available on a Navistar FC3800 chassis.

Promotion for a school bus manufacturer.

AGENCY:
Young & Laramore,
Indianapolis, Indiana

CREATIVE DIRECTORS:
David Young,
Jeff Laramore

ART DIRECTOR:
Chris Beatty

ILLUSTRATOR:
Scott Montgomery

PHOTOGRAPHERS:
Greg Whitaker,
Dale Bernstein

COPYWRITER:
Nina Anthony

PRODUCTION:
Dale Bernstein

QUANTITY: 10,000

PRINTING PROCESS:
Offset

1994 cruise atlas.

DESIGN FIRM:

Pentagram Design,

San Francisco, California

ART DIRECTOR:

Neil Shakery

PHOTOGRAPHERS:

Harvey Lloyd,

John Blaustein

Royal Viking Line (Cruise Line)

What can we do to delight the world's most discerning travelers? Everything! And we do. The liveliest minds engage and entertain you in our 1994 World Affairs Program. Our onboard concierge arranges for tickets to a sold-out show in your next port. Through our Celebrity Chefs Program, fine culinary masters, such as Paul Bocuse and Jeremiah Tower, create exquisite cuisine. There are parties, movies, bridge, golf instruction and light-hearted classes in everything from arranging flowers to arranging the stress right out of your life.

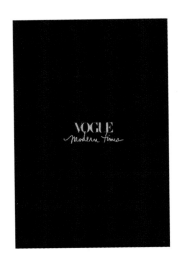

Promotion targeted to advertisers.

ART DIRECTOR:

Juan Gallardo/

Vogue Promotion,

New York, New York

DESIGNER/HAND

LETTERER: Nancy Arnold

PHOTOGRAPHER:

John Huba

Style is instinctive to the Vogue reader.

It's the way she lives her life.

Promotion for Expression Prairie paper line.

AGENCY:

Northlich Stolley LaWarre, Cincinnati, Ohio

ART DIRECTOR:

Joe Stryker

CREATIVE DIRECTOR:

Don Perkins

COPYWRITER: Bob Guard

QUANTITY: 15,000

PRINTING PROCESS:

Offset; "X" was die-cut through entire brochure after assembly.

Design guidelines/
specifications for use of
the logo on any type of
communication.

DESIGN FIRM:

Siegel & Gale, Inc.,

New York, New York

CREATIVE DIRECTOR:

Kenneth R. Cooke

ASSOCIATE DESIGN

DIRECTOR: Sondra Adams

BUDGET: $150,000

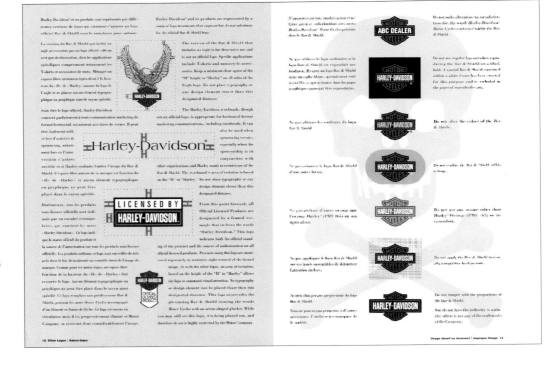

Exhibitor sales prospectus for New York Premier Collections.

DESIGN FIRM:

Kappa Graphic Design Studio, Inc.,

Fort Lee, New Jersey

ART DIRECTORS/ DESIGNERS:

Maddalena Gracis, Gianluigi Giulianelli

PHOTOGRAPHER:

Fabrizio Ferri

QUANTITY: 5000

PRINTING PROCESS:

Stonetone printing

 designerwear

diffusion

swimwear

accessories

Capabilities brochure.

DESIGN FIRM:

Rood Mort Design,

Portland, Oregon;

Ziba Design

ART DIRECTOR/

DESIGNER: Don Rood

PRINCIPAL

PHOTOGRAPHY:

Micheal Jones

Photography

TYPOGRAPHY:

Studio Source

PRINTER:

Dynagraphics, Inc.

COLOR SEPARATIONS/

FILM PREP:

Color Technology

QUANTITY: 2500

PRINTING PROCESS:

Cover: letterpress;

interior: lithography

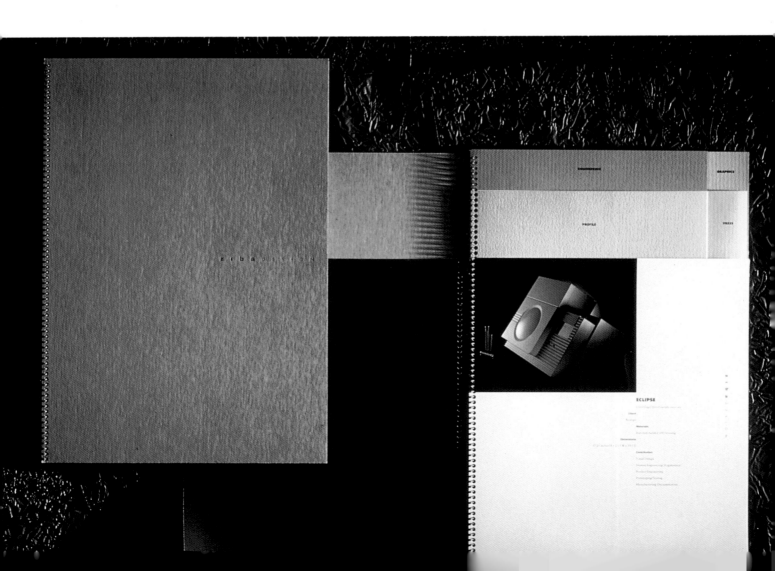

Annual direct-mail self-promotion.

DESIGN FIRM:

Pitcock Design Group,

South Bend, Indiana

ART DIRECTOR/

DESIGNER/ILLUSTRATOR:

Tom Pitcock

RESEARCH/

COPY DEVELOPMENT:

Kathleen Desmond

BUDGET: $1062

QUANTITY: 250

PRINTING PROCESS:

Offset

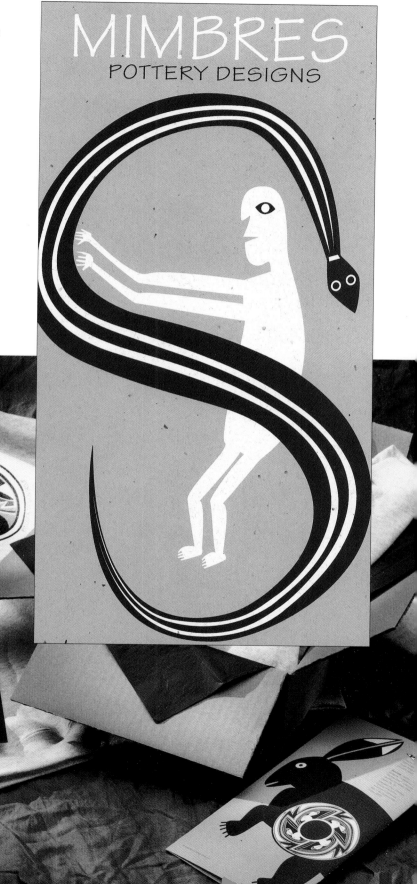

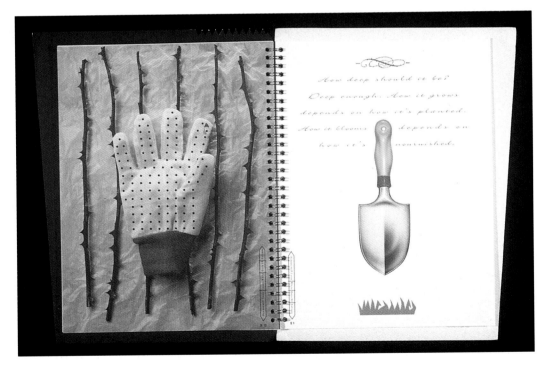

Promotion for opaque and

cover paper lines.

DESIGN FIRM: Royal,

Memphis, Tennessee

DESIGNER/ILLUSTRATOR:

Royal

PHOTOGRAPHER:

Allen Mims

COPYWRITER:

Dan Conaway

PRODUCTION:

Greatlakes Litho

BUDGET: $40,000

QUANTITY: 50,000

PRINTING PROCESS:

4-color, match colors,

die-cutting, embossing,

foil-stamping

Paper promotion.

DESIGN FIRM:

Monadnock Paper Mills,

Bennington,

New Hampshire

DESIGNER: Joel Katz

ARTISTS: Jeff Brice,

Scott Morgan, Jenny Lynn,

Steven Guarnaccia, John

Hersey, Michael Northrup,

Edward Matalon, Lance

Hidy, Steven Lyons

PRODUCTION:

Strine Printing

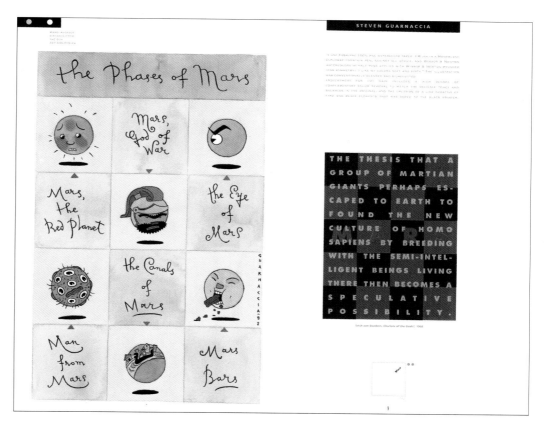

Monadnock Paper Mills, Inc.

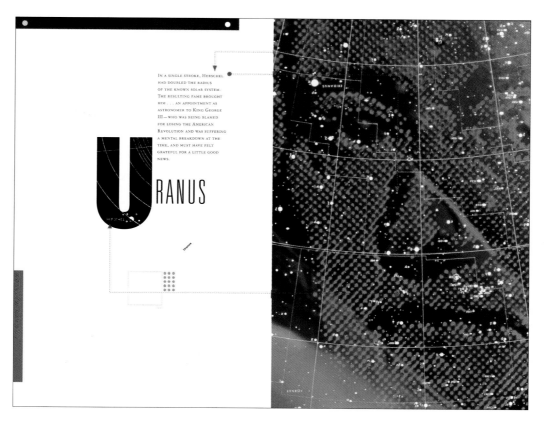

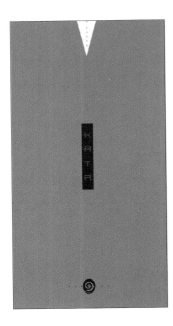

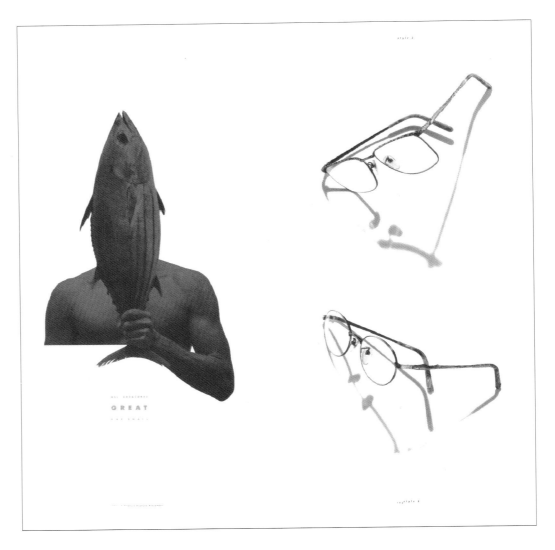

Catalog.

DESIGN FIRM:

Studio Seireeni,

Los Angeles, California

CREATIVE DIRECTOR:

Rick Seireeni

ART DIRECTOR/

DESIGNER/ILLUSTRATOR:

Romane Cameron

PHOTOGRAPHER: Amedeo

PRODUCTION MANAGER:

Jim Pezzullo

BUDGET: $25,000

QUANTITY: 5000

PRINTING PROCESS:

Cover: 1-color plus foil over

one PMS color; text: 4-color

Wilshire Designs (Fashion Eyewear)

Paper promotion.

DESIGN FIRM:

The Kuester Group,

Minneapolis, Minnesota

ART DIRECTOR:

Kevin B. Kuester

DESIGNERS: Tim Sauer,

Kevin B. Kuester

COPYWRITER:

David Forney

QUANTITY: 70,000

PRINTING PROCESS:

4-color

Potlatch Corporation (Paper Manufacturer)

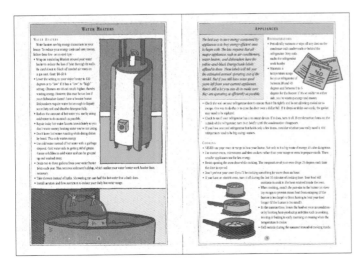

Series of energy-saving guides targeted to various audiences.

DESIGN FIRM:

Oddo Design,

Houston, Texas

CREATIVE DIRECTOR:

Dale Fournier

DESIGNER/ILLUSTRATOR:

Tommy Oddo

COPYWRITER: Pam Roark

PRINTING PROCESS:

Offset lithography

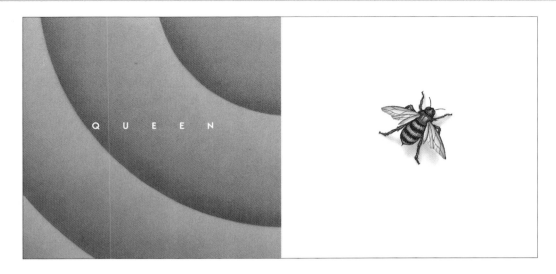

QUEEN

MONARCH

Promotion for Regalia

paper line.

DESIGN FIRM: Royal,

Memphis, Tennessee

DESIGNER/ILLUSTRATOR/

COPYWRITER: Royal

COPY INTRODUCTION:

Dan Conaway

PRODUCTION: Washburn

Graphics, Inc.

BUDGET: $12,000

QUANTITY: 35,000

PRINTING PROCESS:

4-color

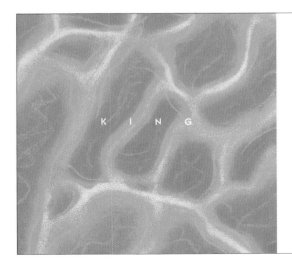

KING

Catalog.

DESIGN FIRM:

Robson & Associates,

Rowayton, Connecticut

ART DIRECTOR/

DESIGNER: Jack Robson

PHOTOGRAPHERS:

Michael Furman, Gregg

Pease, John Kelly, Jim

Stafford, Tracey Kroll,

Jack Robson

SCANNING/CRISTAL

RASTER SEPARATIONS:

Tana Color Graphics

PRINTER: Lebanon Valley

Offset

BUDGET: $113,000

QUANTITY: 26,000

PRINTING PROCESS:

Offset

Serotta Sports, Inc. (Competition Road Bicycles)

Catalog.

DESIGN FIRM:

Pentagram Design,

San Francisco, California

ART DIRECTOR:

Lowell Williams

DESIGNERS:

Melinda Maniscalco,

Mark Selfe

Williams-Sonoma (Housewares)

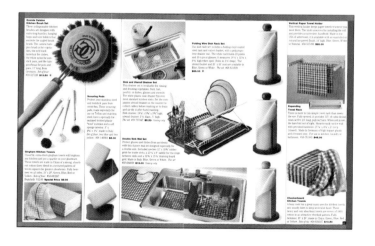

Paper promotion.

DESIGN FIRM:

Besser Joseph Partners,

Santa Monica, California

ART DIRECTORS:

Douglas Joseph, Rik Besser

DESIGNERS:

Besser Joseph Partners

ILLUSTRATORS:

Thom Sevalrud, Sudi

McCollum, Richard Downs

BUDGET: $25,000

QUANTITY: 30,000

PRINTING PROCESS:

Embossing, lithography

and thermography

Each Loftus house is sited to take maximum advantage of the location while best showing the aesthetic detail of the structure. ❧ Here the pond was originally bordered by steep rolling hills. The solution was excavating, then terracing the house into the hill with stone walls. This gives integrity and privacy to the house and grounds while letting the house stand proudly above and behind the pond. ❧ The stone facade reflects the terracing below and was laid with lime mortar in the traditional way to create a warm contrast to the formal entrance. ❧

People often ask if Loftus Associates build Georgian houses or Federal houses. "I tell them that we design New England Colonial houses. This covers a lot of ground because the houses in New England bridge different architectural eras. Our work shares

with them a dignity and sense of proportion that is rarely found in private homes today." ❧ Here an elegant curved Colonial staircase with carved stringer brackets has raised starting newell, custom railings and balusters. ❧ The delicate carved wooden mantle above is modeled after the Federal period. ❧

Paper promotion for Superfine and Artemis papers and self-promotion for John Loftus Associates, home builders.

DESIGN FIRM:
Hawthorne/Wolfe, Inc.,
St. Louis, Missouri
ART DIRECTOR/
DESIGNER: Doug Wolfe
PHOTOGRAPHER:
Cheryl Pendleton

Re-
thinking
Design

The inside front and back covers depict subjects in Stanley Milgram's experiments on obedience at Yale University in the early sixties.

The subject on the inside front cover is administering an electric shock in Experiment 4: Touch Proximity Condition. The subject on the inside back cover is shown breaking off the experiment.

"Redesigning Thinking" is courtesy of a fax from Erik Spiekermann, MetaDesign, Berlin.

Rethinking Design: New ways of looking at what designers do and why they do it from Mohawk

Promotion for line of recycled papers.

DESIGN FIRM: Pentagram Design, New York, New York

ART DIRECTOR: Michael Bierut

DESIGNERS: Michael Bierut, Lisa Cerveny

CONTRIBUTING DESIGNERS: P. Scott Makela, Dana Arnett

PHOTOGRAPHERS: John Paul Endress, Tom Strong

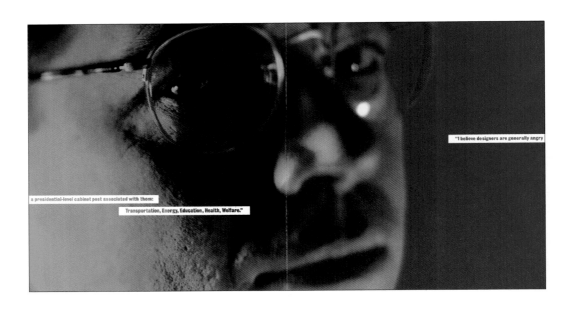

"I believe designers are generally angry

a presidential-level cabinet post associated with them:

Transportation, Energy, Education, Health, Welfare."

JustSayN

Mohawk Paper Mills

Promotion for Vellum

papers.

DESIGN FIRM:

Pentagram Design,

New York, New York

ART DIRECTOR/

COPYWRITER:

Michael Bierut

DESIGNER: Lisa Cerveny

PHOTOGRAPHER:

John Paul Endress

COORDINATOR:

Karla Coe

PRINTER:

Diversified Graphics

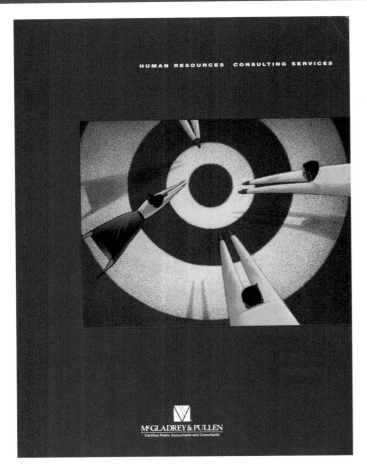

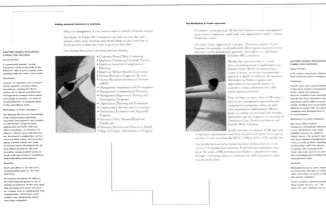

Series of capabilities brochures.

ILLUSTRATOR:

David Tillinghast,

South Pasadena, California

AGENCY:

Welsh & Associates

ART DIRECTOR:

Francoise Willems

BUDGET: $1500 each

cover (illustration only)

A SPECIAL RESPONSIBILITY

Global

Community

Environmental

Excellence

Johnson & Johnson

Capabilities brochure.

AGENCY:

Burson Marsteller,

Woodinville, Washington

DESIGNER: Shari Finger

ILLUSTRATOR:

George Y. Abe

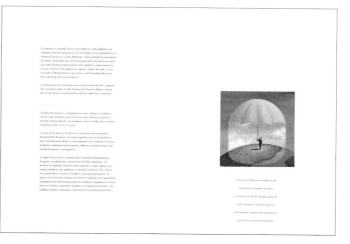

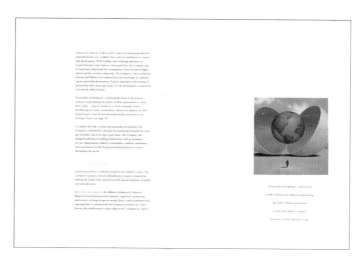

Promotion for pen-based computer.

DESIGN FIRM:

Natalie Kitamura Design,

San Francisco, California

AGENCY:

Woolward and Partners

ART DIRECTORS:

Natalie Kitamura,

Jorgen Grann

DESIGNER:

Catherine Wong

ILLUSTRATOR:

Ward Schumaker

PHOTOGRAPHERS:

Bob Mizono, Christian

Peacock, Barry Robinson

QUANTITY: 50,000

PRINTING PROCESS:

Sheet fed

HOW TO *keep* FROM SHOWING UP *under-equipped.*

All you need to know, instantly, with EO.

You can keep forms or files in EO's memory, and check off or add items with a stroke of the pen. Thousands upon thousands of pages of product catalogues, pricing sheets, and client lists are all at your fingertips: you can simply download them into EO from any PC compatible by a direct cable hookup, or carry them on lightweight RAM expansion cards. And if you find yourself in the field without a vital piece of information, you can retrieve it (via the high speed data modem) from your desktop PC or any PC-compatible network system, or have it faxed to you from anywhere.

As you're talking to a client, you can call up an order form, fill it out, check it against a current inventory file, and fax it to distribution. And the pen-based interface means that you can get the client's signature right on your EO. Not only is the order on its way before you've left the client's office, but you'll have less paperwork to do when you get back to yours.

EO includes Pensoft Personal Perspective, an intuitive personal organizer that includes a calendar, address book, electronic notepad, and a daily to-do list that carries over unfinished projects. EO will remind you to "call Harry" every day until you get around to it, and then a simple checkmark will remove it from future lists, while saving it for your reference. And by highlighting "Harry", you can call up all the previous entries that involve him. You have instant access to every note you've ever taken, without having to thumb through an appointment book. And if you want to know his home phone number or favorite Beatle, you can keep a record of that, too.

HOW TO OUTFIT *your* GROUP FOR BETTER *performance, instantly.*

Effective field force automation, with EO.

Cases cited in the Harvard Business Review show that sales force automation typically brings a 10% to 30% increase in sales. When one large electronics firm automated its sales force, sales rose 33%, productivity rose 31%, and sales force attrition dropped 40% in the first year alone. Seven out of ten respondents to a Sales & Marketing Management survey believe computer applications give marketers a competitive edge. However, because of the highly personal and interactive nature of sales, automation is often awkward.

EO is designed to overcome that awkwardness. The intuitive pen-based interface lets users jot things down naturally, and the cellular phone and fax are as easy to operate as their conventional counterparts. Users can group documents by project, so they work more naturally. And its personal organizational tools mean better time management for a more efficient staff.

The PenPoint operating system is one of the most popular operating systems for pen-based computing, and a wide community of independent software vendors make applications for EO. You can use EO fresh from the package to turn your current forms into electronic order sheets, and your files into portable client profiles. Because of its instant usability, EO's payback can come much more quickly than with laptops, which require specialized configurations and applications. And immediate implementation means immediate feedback from users, which speeds the design of custom applications that will make your system as efficient as possible. EO's all-in-one configuration also means that communication and computing solutions can be implemented simultaneously, rather than in separate rounds of testing and development.

AT&T EO (Pen-Based Personal Computer)

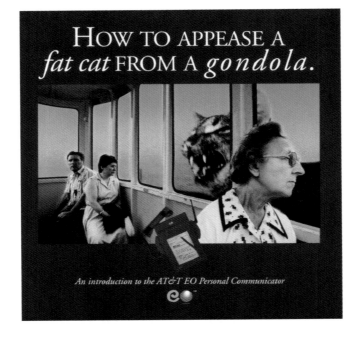

An introduction to the AT&T EO Personal Communicator

One of a series of "decade" booklets done as class project at Montana State University, Bozeman, Montana.

ART DIRECTOR:

Anne Garner/The Bozarts Press, Bozeman, Montana

DESIGNERS:

Devon Baker (cover),

Theresa DePuydt (1941),

Jaine Naylor (1944),

Shawna Kalitowski (Peace)

ILLUSTRATORS:

Devon Baker (cover),

Robert T. McCall (1941)

BUDGET: $874 divided among student participants

QUANTITY: 200

PRINTING PROCESS:

Multilith

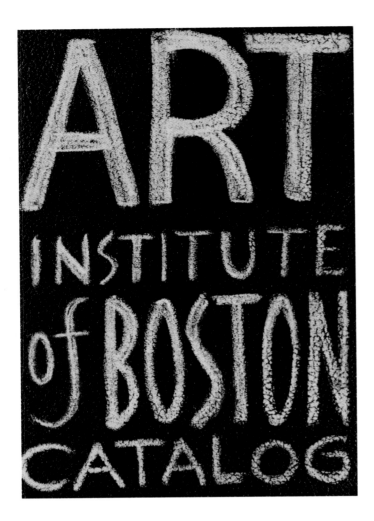

Course catalog.

DESIGN FIRM:

Big Blue Dot,

Watertown, Massachusetts

ART DIRECTOR: Scott Nash

DESIGNER/LETTERER:

Tim Nihoff

Art Institute of Boston

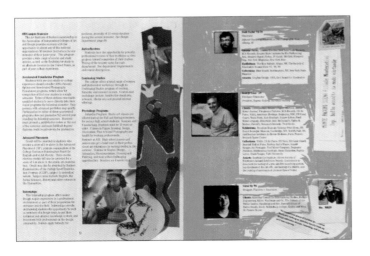

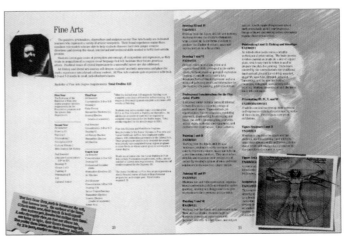

Promotion for a two-man

theatrical group.

DESIGNER: Art Chantry

PHOTOGRAPHER:

Kevin Lohman

BUDGET: Design: $200;

Printing: $200

QUANTITY: 1500–2000

PRINTING PROCESS:

Newspaper, web offset

Nemzoff/Roth (Artist Management)

Three-part direct-mail promotion to attract business meetings to Chicago suburb of Oak Brook.

DESIGN FIRM:

Gams Chicago, Inc., Chicago, Illinois

DESIGNER:

John V. Anderson

COPYWRITER:

Randy Siegal

BUDGET: Film and printing: $17,900

QUANTITY: 3000 of each

PRINTING PROCESS:

Offset, 1-color on 10-point C2S Kromekote; diecut

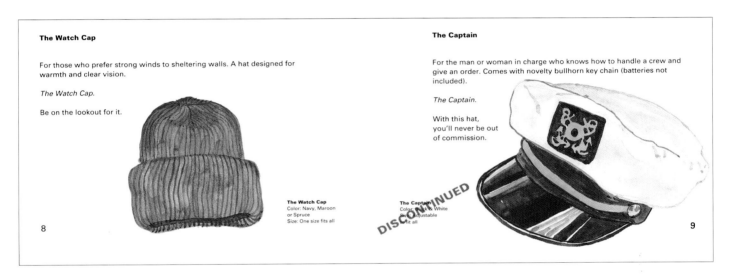

The Holmes

For the person who looks beyond mere appearances. A brilliant deduction of a hat, in classic black-and-white houndstooth.

The Holmes.

It would be a crime
not
to
get
one.

The Holmes
Color: Black-and-white
Sizes: S, M, L, XL

4

The Coachman

For the person who's not afraid to stand out. Not for yes-women or yes-men. In black or, understandably, red.

The Coachman.

Outstandingly stylish.

The Coachman
Color: Black or Red
Sizes: M & L

5

The Watch Cap

For those who prefer strong winds to sheltering walls. A hat designed for warmth and clear vision.

The Watch Cap.

Be on the lookout for it.

The Watch Cap
Color: Navy, Maroon or Spruce
Size: One size fits all

8

The Captain

For the man or woman in charge who knows how to handle a crew and give an order. Comes with novelty bullhorn key chain (batteries not included).

The Captain.

With this hat,
you'll never be out
of commission.

The Captain
Color: Black & White
Size: Adjustable
One size fits all

DISCONTINUED

9

Aetna (Insurance/Financial Services)

"Hats Off"

Hat Catalog

Catalog of hats for internal incentive program. Selected employees, nominated by colleagues or customers, chose a hat as the symbol of their "crowning achievement."

DESIGN FIRM:
Peter Good Graphic Design, Chester, Connecticut

ART DIRECTORS:
Susan Beaumier, Amy Day Kahn

DESIGNER:
Susan Beaumier

ILLUSTRATOR:
David Schultz

COPYWRITERS:
Ernie Mills, Amy Day Kahn

BUDGET: $15,000

QUANTITY: 2000

PRINTING PROCESS:
Offset, 4-color

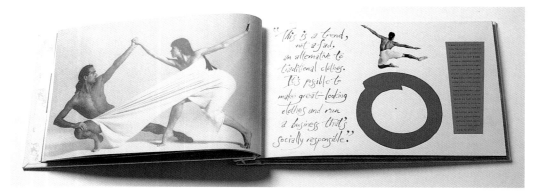

Sales promotion targeted
to retailers.
DESIGN FIRM:
Detour Design,
New York, New York
ART DIRECTORS:
Gretchen Van Der Grinten,
Nick Van Der Grinten
PHOTOGRAPHER:
Davies & Starr,
Bruce Davidson,
Andreas Bleckman
QUANTITY: 300
PRINTING PROCESS:
Offset—1-, 2- and 4-color,
hand assembled

O Wear (Fashion)

Uh Oh Clothing (Fashion)

Direct-mail promotion.

DESIGN FIRM:

Campbell Fisher Ditko

Design, Phoenix, Arizona

ART DIRECTOR:

Steve Ditko

DESIGNERS: Steve Ditko,

Mike Campbell

ILLUSTRATOR:

Rick Rusing

COPYWRITER: Jill Spear

BUDGET: $30,000

QUANTITY: 3200

PRINTING PROCESS:

4-color dryography and

1-color dryography

Sales promotion.

DESIGN FIRM:

Michael Brock Design,

Los Angeles , California

ART DIRECTOR:

Michael Brock

DESIGNERS: Michael

Brock, Daina H. Kemp

PHOTOGRAPHER:

Paul Jonason

QUANTITY: 1000

PRINTING PROCESS:

Offset

Fred Sands (Real Estate)

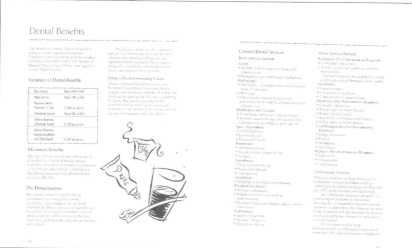

Nordstrom (Department Store)

Employee personal benefits booklets.

ART DIRECTOR:

Cheryl Zahniser/

Nordstrom Advertising/

Seattle, Washington

DESIGNER:

Alison Kan Grevstad

ILLUSTRATORS:

Susan Gross, Philippe

Lardy, Craig Smallish,

Ward Schumaker

LOGO DESIGNER:

Kurt Hollomon/

Sandstrom Design

PRINTER: United

Graphics

QUANTITY: 36,000

PRINTING PROCESS:

Offset lithography

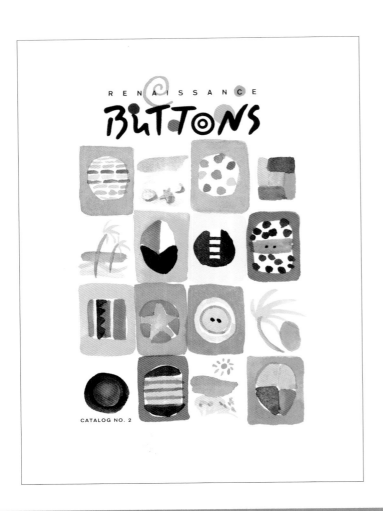

Catalog for a wholesaler of buttons made of natural materials.

DESIGN FIRM:

Maxine Boll,

Lambertville, New Jersey

ART DIRECTOR/

DESIGNER/ILLUSTRATOR:

Maxine Boll

QUANTITY: 10,000

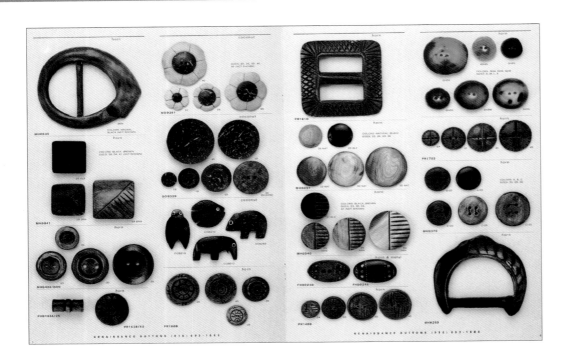

Informational brochure for

first-time home-buyers.

DESIGN FIRM:

Sibley/Peteet Design,

Dallas, Texas

CREATIVE DIRECTOR:

Brent Ladd/GSD&M

ART DIRECTOR/

DESIGNER: Rex Peteet

ILLUSTRATOR:

Linda Helton

COPYWRITER: GSD&M

AGENCY: GSD&M

QUANTITY: 1,000,000

PRINTING PROCESS: Web

Fannie Mae (Home Mortgage Financing)

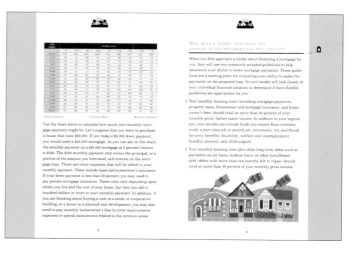

Capabilities brochure for a
public relations firm
specializing in hi-tech clients.
DESIGN FIRM:
Deborah Berry Design,
San Rafael, California
ART DIRECTOR:
Deborah Berry
DESIGNER:
Deborah Berry
ILLUSTRATOR:
Darrel Kolosta
COPYWRITER:
John Frazier
PRODUCTION:
Lisa La Prath
TYPOGRAPHY:
Rapid Typograhpers
BUDGET: 20,000
QUANTITY: 10,000
PRINTING PROCESS:
Offset lithography

Cunningham Communications, Inc.

COMMUNICATION COMPONENTS *provides high-quality, affordable solutions for small and emerging companies. It avails you of our high technology expertise without the expenses incurred by our full-service clients.* WE *combine the essential ele-* *ments of strategic communication in a cost-effective, six-month pro- gram. These are the same services we provide our larger clients, there are just fewer of them.* AND *if there's still more to be done after six months, we can arrange another six months to do the things we couldn't address the first time around.*

COMPANIES *come to us because they need help. In most cases, companies come to us because they think they have a public relations problem, which often turns out to be a broader communication issue. But every situation is unique.* TAKE, *for example, the needs of a Fortune 500 company and a company with $2 million in revenue. The smaller firm doesn't have the same communication concerns. Nor should it. But we realize that its problems and opportunities are every bit as important. In either case, they need strategic communication.*

Self-promotion.

DESIGN FIRM:

Firehouse 101 Design,

Columbus, Ohio

DESIGNER:

Terry Alan Rohrbach

BUDGET: $100

QUANTITY: 25

PRINTING PROCESS:

Laserwriter

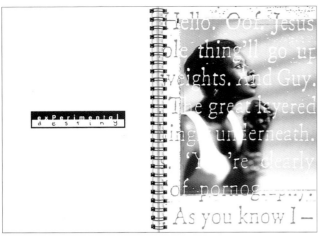

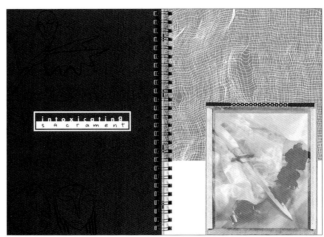

Self-promotion.

DESIGN FIRM:

Firehouse 101 Design,

Columbus, Ohio

CREATIVE DIRECTOR:

Charles Wagner

ART DIRECTOR/

DESIGNER/ILLUSTRATOR:

Kirk Richard Smith

PHOTOGRAPHER:

Will Shively

COPYWRITER:

Doug Burdick

PRINTER: J.F. Hopkins

BUDGET: Donated printing,

separations, graphic design,

photography

QUANTITY: 3000

PRINTING PROCESS:

4-process colors plus

PMS 874 plus varnish

Self-promotion targeting magazines and record companies.

DESIGN FIRM:
Firehouse 101 Design, Columbus, Ohio

ART DIRECTOR/
ILLUSTRATOR:
Kirk Richard Smith

PRINTER: J.F. Hopkins

SEPARATIONS: Lash Litho

BUDGET: $2500

QUANTITY: 3000

PRINTING PROCESS:
4-color plus varnish

Firehouse 101 Design

I am certain of nothing but of the holiness of the Hearts affections and the truth of Imagination- what the imagination seizes as beauty must be truth, whether it existed before or not.

j. keats

Point-of-purchase sales promotion.

AGENCY:

Team One Advertising,

New York, New York

ART DIRECTOR:

Scott Bremner

PHOTOGRAPHER:

Craig Cutler

QUANTITY: 200,000

PRINTING PROCESS:

4-color plus PMS plus

dull varnish

Lexus (Luxury Automobiles)

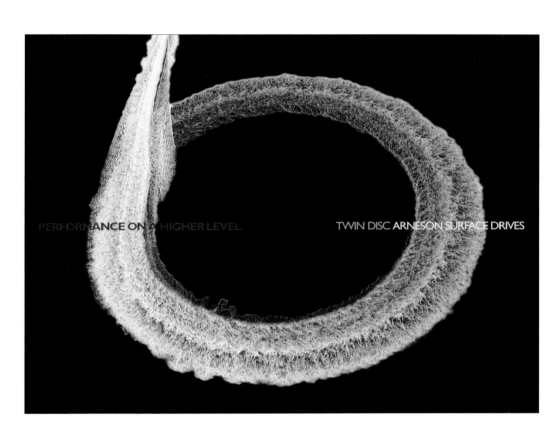

Capabilities brochure.

AGENCY: Stahl Design Inc.,

Indianapolis, Indiana

AGENCY:

Quinlan Advertising

ART DIRECTOR/

DESIGNER: David Stahl

PHOTOGRAPHER:

John Fleck,

Drew Endicott

ILLUSTRATOR:

Greg LaFever,

COPYWRITER:

John McCail

BUDGET: $40,000

QUANTITY: 4000

PRINTING PROCESS:

4-color plus one match

color plus gloss varnish

overall

Twin Disc, Inc. (Power Transmission Equipment Manufacturer)

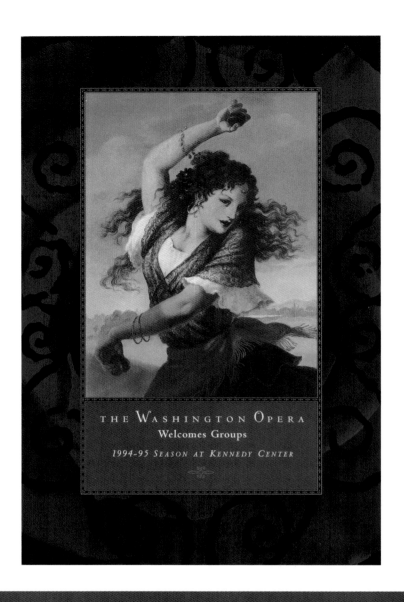

1994 season guide.

DESIGN FIRM: May & Co.,

Dallas, Texas

ART DIRECTOR:

Douglas May

DESIGNER:

Candace Buchanan Morgan

ILLUSTRATOR:

Kinuko Craft (cover)

PHOTOMONTAGES:

J. Stewart Huey

BUDGET: 75,000

QUANTITY: 100,000

PRINTING PROCESS:

6/6 offset, perfect bind

Brochure promoting the season's events.

DESIGN FIRM:
Hansen Design Company, Seattle, Washington

ART DIRECTOR/
DESIGNER: Pat Hansen

ILLUSTRATORS:
Greg Stadler, Pat Hansen

COVER PHOTO:
Dick Busher

PRINTER:
Graphic Arts Center

BUDGET: $8000

QUANTITY: 115,000

PRINTING PROCESS:
4-color with eight color tint builds, recycled paper

The 5th Avenue Musical Theatre Company

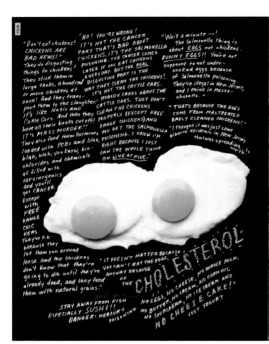

One of a series of "Subjective Reasoning" paper promotions.

DESIGN FIRM:

Pentagram Design, New York, New York

ART DIRECTORS:

Paula Scher, Bill Drenttel

DESIGNERS: Paula Scher, Ron Louie

ILLUSTRATOR:

Paula Scher

COPYWRITERS:

Tony Hendra, Paula Scher

COORDINATOR:

Melissa Hoffman

TYPOGRAPHER:

Typogram

PRINTER:

Lebanon Valley Offset

The single biggest ecological issue is acid-rain. The single biggest ecological crisis is the disappearance of the rain-forest. The single biggest obligation of the environmental movement is to educate people about the consequences of 'convenience." The single most urgent ecological issue is eradicating fossil-fuels. The single most important ecological issue is saving the oceans. The single most explosive environmental issue is nuclear technology. The single most urgent environmental need is the development of alternative fuels.

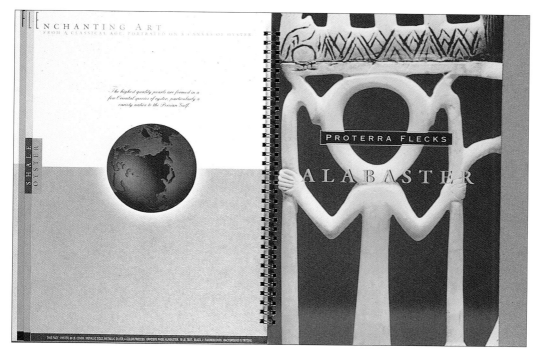

Paper promotion.

DESIGN FIRM:

Antista Design, Inc.,

Atlanta, Georgia

ART DIRECTOR/

DESIGNER: Tom Antista

PHOTOGRAPHERS:

Roger Macuch,

Rick Vanderpool,

Giorgio Palmisano

COPYWRITERS:

Jolene Pierson Perry,

Antista Design, Inc.

QUANTITY: 70,000

PRINTING PROCESS:

4-color plus match colors,

metallic colors and

fluorescent colors.

Hopper Paper

Experienced account service representatives ensure your RxChoice mail service program is quickly and efficiently implemented. These professionals then use detailed management data to monitor RxChoice's ongoing performance, making certain your cost containment and service goals are enhanced.

DRUG UTILIZATION REVIEW RxChoice's drug utilization review (DUR) process includes prospective, concurrent and retrospective monitoring.

PROSPECTIVE DUR RxChoice's Preferred Drug Formulary is the centerpiece of all prospective DUR activities, ensuring cost and quality controls are enacted prior to prescription dispensing.

The Preferred Drug Formulary reduces prescription cost while delivering equal or better patient outcome. This goal is attained through a systematic process of claims review and clinical intervention, ensuring all drug therapy is safe, cost effective and appropriate. Compliance to the Preferred Drug Formulary is achieved by continuously monitoring physician prescribing.

CONCURRENT DUR Concurrent DUR edits, improving quality of care and cost savings, include drug-drug interaction, therapeutic duplication, drug-disease interaction, drug-dose age analysis, excessive/insufficient dosing, excessive utilization and drug-pregnancy interaction.

Diagnostek, Inc. (Diversified Pharmacy Management)

detailed management reports generated monthly, quarterly and annually, allow ongoing performance assessment and improved, proactive decision making. Standard and ad hoc reports deliver utilization, operational and financial data, enhancing Plan design flexibility.

RETROSPECTIVE DUR Retrospective DUR focuses on physician prescribing and employee profiling.

PHYSICIAN PRESCRIBING Physician prescribing, monitored by the Department of Clinical Pharmacy, targets areas where physician education can improve quality of care and cost efficiency. Computerized analysis identifies utilization that is statistically different from national and group norms for a therapeutic class. Cost trends per therapeutic class, physician group or physician are also evaluated.

PHYSICIAN EDUCATION Prescriptions are analyzed for excessive dosing, employee over-utilization, employee specific criteria, formulary non-compliance and physician tendency to prescribe high cost medications. Aberrant physician prescribing is identified through internal reports and clinical review. Educational strategies are then implemented to improve prescribing behavior.

EMPLOYEE PROFILING Employee profiles are reviewed quarterly. RxChoice screens employee profiles for excessive utilization, excessive monthly drug expenditures, drug-disease conflicts and formulary non-compliance. Employee profiles are reviewed by the Department of Clinical Pharmacy to determine utilization improvement.

Promotional brochure for Rx Choice, a mail service pharmacy program.

DESIGN FIRM: Kilmer, Kilmer & James, Inc., Albuquerque, New Mexico

ART DIRECTORS/ DESIGNERS: Richard Kilmer, Brenda Kilmer

PHOTOGRAPHER: Michael Barley

COPYWRITER: David Jones

COMPUTER ARTIST: Marc Swindle

QUANTITY: 7500

PRINTING PROCESS: Cover: letterpress; inside: 4-color plus varnish

Promotion targeted to prospective business clients.

DESIGN FIRM:

Roger Christian & Co

San Antonio, Texas

DESIGNER:

Roger Christian

ILLUSTRATOR:

Keith Graves

PRINTING:

Padgett Printing

BUDGET: Approximately $18,000

QUANTITY: 5000

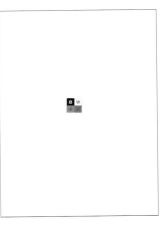

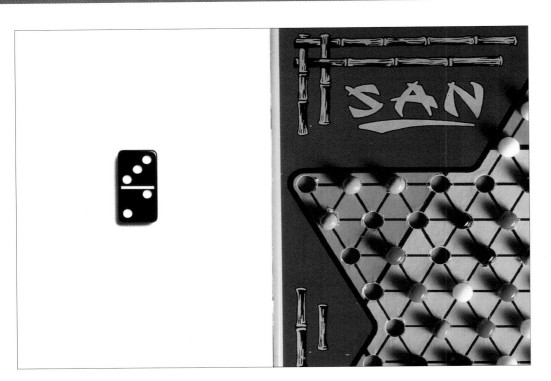

Self-promotion.

DESIGN FIRM:

Tom Hair Marketing Design,

Houston, Texas

ART DIRECTOR/

DESIGNER/ILLUSTRATOR:

Tom Hair

PHOTOGRAPHER:

Pete Lacker

4

5

10

11

Promotion for Innovance
de Mohawk paper line.
DESIGN FIRM:
Liska and Associates,
Chicago, Illinois
ART DIRECTOR:
Steve Liska
DESIGNER: Kim Nyberg
PHOTOGRAPHER:
Charles Shotwell
QUANTITY: 80,000
PRINTING PROCESS:
4-color

Promotion targeted to art buyers.

DESIGN FIRM: May & Co., Dallas, Texas

ART DIRECTOR: Douglas May

ART DIRECTOR: Lynn Bernick

DESIGNER: Candace Buchanan

BUDGET: $45,000

QUANTITY: 15,000

PRINTING PROCESS: 6/6 offset, perfect bind

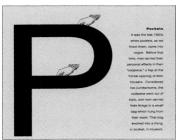
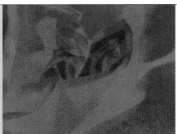

Pockets

It was the late 1500s when pockets, as we know them, came into vogue. Before that time, men carried their personal effects in their "codpiece," a flap at the frontal opening of their trousers. Considered too cumbersome, the codpiece went out of style, and men carried their things in a small bag which hung from their waist. That bag evolved into a lining, or pocket, in trousers.

Buttons

Dating back to about 2000 BC, buttons were first used, not as a means of fastening clothing, but as decorative disks made of shells, ivory, bone and wood, that were sewn on men's and women's clothing. Buttons remained purely ornamental for almost 3500 years until the 13th century when a tailor made a striking discovery and matched a button-hole to a button. Voila!

Paper promotion.

DESIGN FIRM: Siebert Design, Cincinnati, Ohio

ART DIRECTOR: Lori Siebert

DESIGNER: Lisa Ballard

ILLUSTRATORS: Curtis Parker, John Patrick

PHOTOGRAPHER: Bray Ficken

Howard Paper

Pretzels

Of holy origin are pretzels! The crisscross-shaped dough was the creation of a medieval Italian monk who awarded the treat to children for memorizing their prayers. The shape connotes the folded arms of children in prayer. The recipe for pretzels spread to Germany where it was called "bracel," the

Sandwich

John Montagu, the fourth earl of Sandwich, was a notorious 18th-century gambler. He once spent 24 hours straight gambling, ordering that sliced meats and cheeses be served to him between pieces of bread at the gambling table. Doing so allowed him to eat with one hand and gamble with the other. Hence, the sandwich was born.

Everyday Things Made *Extraordinary*

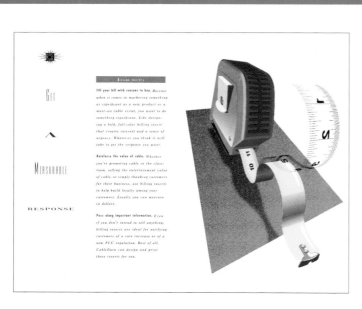

Capabilities brochure.

DESIGN FIRM:

Tackett Barbaria Design,

Sacramento, California

DESIGNER: Dana Kamppila

ILLUSTRATOR:

Patrick Rooney

(tape measure)

PHOTOGRAPHERS:

James Woodson (cover),

Pete McArthur (hammers)

COPYWRITER:

Julie Richardson

BUDGET: $17,500 (design

and printing)

QUANTITY: 5000

PRINTING PROCESS:

Cover: 4-color plus custom-

match metallic PMS plus

gloss varnish, dull spot

varnish and tinted dull spot

varnish/ custom match

metallic PMS (double hit)

plus gloss varnish; inside:

4-color plus PMS plus gloss

varnish

ACS REDUCES YOUR EXPENDITURES. *Outsourcing your data processing operations with ACS makes bottom-line good sense. At minimum, it reduces costs by consolidating your operations with existing ACS facilities and eliminating the redundant functions and the regular capital investments that are necessary to maintain your own data processing environment. Liquidating existing in-house computer assets often provides an additional cash infusion.*

In addition to these basic financial advantages of outsourcing, our clients find that access to our advanced technology can add to overall corporate profits over the long term because of improved computer automation, process control and accountability. Helping clients navigate through the complexities of technology is a case in point. We assisted a nationwide retail chain in evaluating several third-party software packages, purchased the best package, installed it, and continue to operate the system on our hardware. For a nationwide mail-order prescription drug firm, we duplicated an inventory and financial system on our computers while we worked with a Big Six team of software engineers to design a new system on a completely different operating platform. Their consultants even used our facilities to develop and test the new software which provided additional savings.

ACS services your business with multiple hardware platforms and the most advanced software to ensure complete flexibility, adaptability and compatibility.

? **ISSUE:** How can I be sure that outsourcing will save money?

! **SOLUTION:** At ACS we understand that many times cost reduction is your primary objective. In order to show you how outsourcing will save you money, we will work with your people to perform a detailed analysis of your costs. We will then show you line item by line item our plan to reduce your expenses and if you agree with our proposal, we will commit contractually to deliver those savings.

Capabilities brochure.

DESIGN FIRM:

Sibley/Peteet Design,

Dallas, Texas

ART DIRECTOR/

DESIGNER: Rex Peteet

PHOTOGRAPHER:

Klein & Wilson

QUANTITY: 2500

PRINTING PROCESS:

Lithography

Affiliated Computer Systems

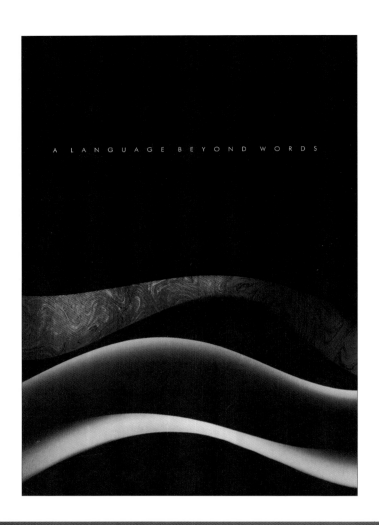

A LANGUAGE BEYOND WORDS

Self-promotion.

DESIGN FIRM:

SHR Design

Communications,

Scottsdale, Arizona

ART DIRECTOR:

Barry Shepard

DESIGNER: Nathan Joseph

PHOTOGRAPHER:

Rick Gayle

COPYWRITER:

Steve Hutchison

Bradley Printing Company

ELEGANCE

It begins with a simplicity of design.

It creates a symmetry of style.

It takes shape through

the clarity of line.

It brightens to

the purity of color.

It results in the integrity of the image.

1994 full line promotional

brochure.

DESIGN FIRM:

SHR Perceptual

Management,

Scottsdale, Arizona

ART DIRECTORS:

Barry Shepard,

Karin Burklein Arnold

DESIGNER:

Karin Burklein Arnold

PHOTOGRAPHERS:

Rick Rusing,

Rodney Rascona

COPYWRITER:

Steve Hutchison

PRODUCTION:

Roger Barger

QUANTITY: 100,000

PRINTING PROCESS:

Sheet-fed

Capabilities brochure for
a provider of software
and printed products.

DESIGN FIRM:

Hornall Anderson
Design Works,
Seattle, Washington

ART DIRECTOR:

Jack Anderson

DESIGNERS:

Jack Anderson,
Heidi Hatlestad,
Bruce Branson-Meyer

PHOTOGRAPHER:

Tom Collicott

COPYWRITER:

Pamela Bond

PRINTING PROCESS:

4-color plus gloss varnish
plus one dull varnish plus
one tinted varnish plus
4 PMS plus dull black

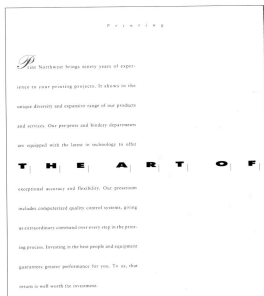

Image brochure.

DESIGN FIRM:

SHR Design

Communications,

Scottsdale, Arizona

ART DIRECTOR:

Barry Shepard

DESIGNER:

Douglas Reeder

PHOTOGRAPHER:

Rodney Rascona

COPYWRITER:

Steve Hutchison

QUANTITY: 10,000

PRINTING PROCESS:

Sheet-fed

Collins Avionics (Avionics Equipment/Systems)

VILLAGE LIFE

Greenwich Village is a little neighborhood in the big city. Home to artists, writers, professionals, and NYU, it's the first love of every New Yorker. Tree-lined streets surround Washington Square Park, where you can roller-skate, play chess, or throw a Frisbee. The Village is famous for its historical landmarks — Greek revival row houses, the Jefferson Market Library, and the Public Theatre — and its not-so-historical ones — the Antique Boutique, the Astor Place Barber Shop, and Tower Records. A lot of what's exciting about New York City is right here, packed into half a square mile that's part myth, part reality. Jazz clubs, sidewalk cafes, and coffeehouses, art galleries, secondhand bookstores, and experimental theatres — all these live here. Today, Greenwich Village may be more middle-class than bohemian, more settled than appears, but the influence of long-gone poets and performers lingers on.

Washington Square Park can be more outdoor reading room, offering folds, or performance space.

STUDENT LIFE

NEW YORK UNIVERSITY

Promotion targeted to prospective students.

ILLUSTRATOR:

Lilla Rogers,

Arlington, Massachusetts

ART DIRECTOR:

Sandy Kaufman

BUDGET: $65,000

QUANTITY: 25,000

PRINTING PROCESS:

Offset

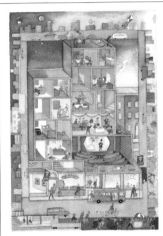

RESIDENCE LIFE

Drop your books, put on a tape, and hang out. Your dorm is home — or the next best thing. It's where you'll have your first adventure living (almost) on your own and where you'll make your closest friends. Over 3,500 undergraduates live on campus, and each residence hall is a little community with its own personality. Some are former hotels — Al Pacino and Jerry Garcia lived in one; Mark Twain in another — and they all have different features: a darkroom, a small theatre, or an exercise room. As a freshman, you'll probably live in a traditional residence hall where it's easy to meet people and make friends. If you like to organize things, you can be part of the committee that runs your dorm. Captain an intramural team or put on a dance. Nobody has to organize pizza parties, late night movies, and study breaks. They just happen all by themselves.

When you live in a dorm, you have to be able your own college decor is a time for study, balance is a time for fun.

SPORTS LIFE

Racquetball, squash, or tennis? How about swimming, running, or weight training? Then the Coles Sports Center is your kind of place. The largest Nautilus and weight-training center on the East Coast, a rooftop track, NCAA-regulation swimming pool and diving tank, fencing salle, and courts for basketball, squash, tennis (indoor and out), and racquetball—Coles has it all. You can choose from UAA variety competition (NCAA—Division III), intramural games, and sports and recreation courses. If you prefer spectator sports, see the best of the best compete at NYU when Coles hosts championship matches: international fencing and international wrestling; NCAA women's basketball; UAA fencing, wrestling, and women's volleyball. If you're into still improvement, learn ball room dancing, master the martial arts, or train for the triathlon. Then collapse in the sauna.

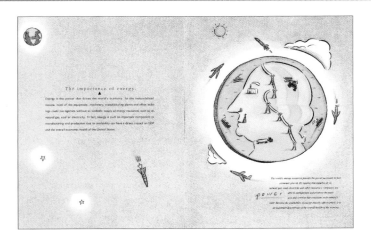

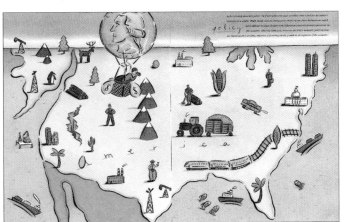

Promotion explaining the Federal Reserve's policy with regard to the energy industry and targeted to that industry.

DESIGN FIRM:

Peterson & Company,

Dallas, Texas

ART DIRECTOR:

Bryan L. Peterson

DESIGNER:

Scott Paramski

ILLUSTRATOR:

Mary Lynn Blassutta

BUDGET: $17,997

PRINTING PROCESS:

Sheet-fed offset

lithography

Promotional series directed

to graphic designers.

DESIGN FIRM:

Pollard Design,

East Hartland, Connecticut

AGENCY: Williams & House

DESIGNERS: Jeff Pollard,

Adrienne Pollard

COVER PHOTOS: Jim Coon

PRINTING PROCESS:

Engraving

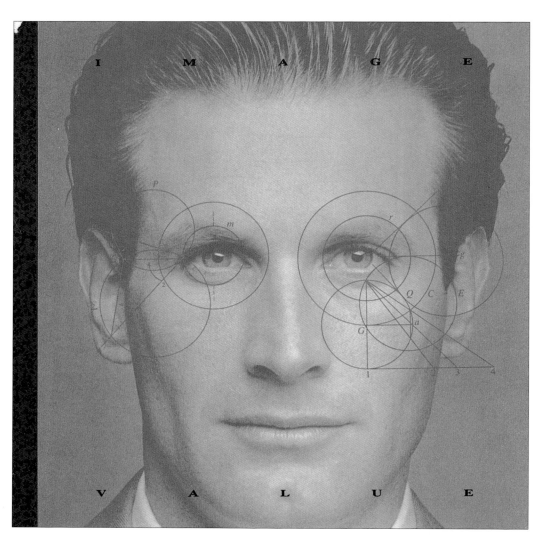

*Above: covers of other
promotions in the series.*

Engraved Stationery

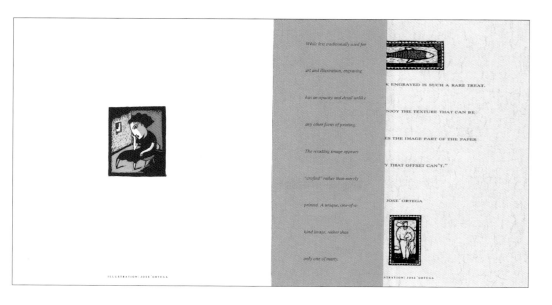

Report on choreographers

in four American cities,

one of a series of reports

commissioned by the

NEA's Research Division.

DESIGN FIRM:

Tom Suzuki, Inc.,

Falls Church, Virginia

ART DIRECTOR:

Tom Suzuki

DESIGNER: Jennifer Long

COVER ILLUSTRATOR:

Jennifer Long (from a

photograph by Marty Sohl)

QUANTITY: 5000

PRINTING PROCESS:

Offset

Photo courtesy Washington Performing Arts Society

In Washington, Asax Joe Drayton almost stands pat for an instant in his modern jazz dance.

Photo courtesy of Washington Performing Arts Society

Chapter 37

General Findings[1]

Demographic Characteristics

Choreographers, like any other clearly defined group of artists, have distinctive characteristics; the typical choreographer is not a typical American. The population at large provides a useful standard of comparison for the survey respondents.[2]

Age. Nearly 60 percent of the survey respondents were in their thirties, a very high concentration compared to 28 percent for the U.S. working age population (aged 22 to 69). Few choreographers in the survey group are younger than 30. Only 15 percent of the survey respondents are 45 or older, compared to 37 percent of the U.S. working age population. The age profiles are shown graphically in Figure 3.1.

Gender. Just under 72 percent of the survey respondents were women. This means that choreography ranks with teaching, nursing and social work as one of the most predominantly female occupations.

Race. Racial and ethnic groups other than whites and Asian Americans were slightly under-represented among the survey respondents, compared to the U.S. population of working age (Figure 3.2). African Americans constitute 11 percent of the U.S. labor force and only 6 percent of the choreographer sample. Hispanics make up 8 percent of the labor force and 4 percent of the sample.[3] It should be noted that 1990 national statistics on 11 artist occupations from the Bureau of Labor Statistics also showed an under-representation of African Americans and Hispanics—at 3.8 percent and 4.3 percent, respectively. Asian Americans represented 5 percent of the choreog-

[1] In this chapter, the number of respondents (out of the 113 total) answering a given question usually is indicated when 100 or more failed to answer that question. Also, no data are presented in situations where the absolute number of respondents in a class is small and few of them answered that particular question.

[2] All the data for the U.S. population are taken from standard federal statistical series, wherever possible from the Statistical Abstract of the United States, 1991, published by the Census Bureau.

[3] The small proportions of African Americans and Hispanics among the respondents was particularly disappointing since special efforts were undertaken to reach them as part of the original study design (see Chapter 2). Clearly, more or different strategies need to be used in future studies to increase response.

Capabilities brochure.

DESIGN FIRM:

Rich Nickel Design, Inc.,

Wheaton, Illinois

ART DIRECTOR:

Rich Nickel

DESIGNER/ILLUSTRATOR:

Dale Janzen

PHOTOGRAPHER:

Richard Mack

PRINTER: Bruce Offset

QUANTITY: 20,000

PRINTING PROCESS:

Cover: embossing and

engraving; inside: offset

GATX (Shipping/Storage)

Photo by Dave Irmiter

Capabilities brochure.

DESIGN FIRM:

Duffy Design,

Minneapolis, Minnesota

CREATIVE DIRECTOR:

Chuck Carlson

ART DIRECTOR/

DESIGNER: Kobe

PRINTER/SEPARATOR:

Print Craft

PRINTING PROCESS:

Lithography

Phillips Beverage

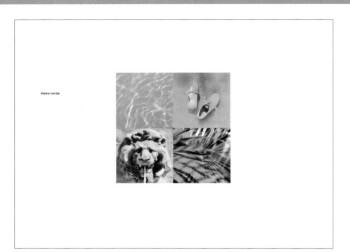

mesa verde

Promotional brochure for
Mesa Verde development.
DESIGN FIRM:
Evans & Associates,
Dallas, Texas, Plano, Texas
DESIGNER: Joe Goodwin
ART DIRECTOR/

DESIGNER: Tim Evans
PHOTOGRAPHER:
Richard Seagraves
BUDGET: $30,000
QUANTITY: 7000
PRINTING PROCESS:
5/5 offset-quadratones

Home court advantage.

Offer all of the winning options when your friends come over to play.

Courtside to poolside; you'll rejuvenate, relax, refresh body and spirit.

home is

Home is where you hang your hat. Where you hail from. You make

yourself at home. It's where you call when you're away. Your home

is your castle, a spot for coffee in the morning and a fire at night.

Home is where the heart is. There's no place like home. Sweet home.

Direct-mail promotion.

DESIGN FIRM:

Wages Design,

Dallas, Texas

CREATIVE DIRECTOR:

Bob Wages

DESIGNER: Lisa Reichrath

PHOTOGRAPHER:

Neal Farris

BUDGET: $50,000

QUANTITY: 20,000

PRINTING PROCESS:

4-color

THE subtle POWER OF NATURE AND THE BEAUTY OF ITS enduring DESIGN. THE epitome OF CLASSIC DESIGN: COLOR, TEXTURE AND PATTERN COMBINED IN A natural SETTING.

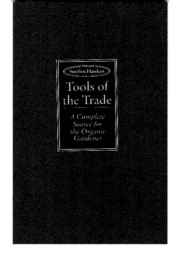

Tool catalog.

DESIGN FIRM:

Sandra McHenry Design,

San Francisco, California

CREATIVE DIRECTORS:

Bonnie Dahan,

Kathy Tierny,

Roger Bergen, Jack Allen

ART DIRECTOR:

Sandra McHenry

DESIGNERS:

Sandra McHenry,

Toby Salk, Hilary Davis

ILLUSTRATOR:

Jim Anderson

PHOTOGRAPHERS:

Sean Sullivan, Jim Sadlon,

David Belda, Doug Menuez

PHOTOGRAPHY

COORDINATOR:

Melinda Lawson

COPYWRITERS:

Evan Elliot,

Deborah Bishop

PRINTING PROCESS:

Web and sheet-fed,

debossed cover

HOES

If you think about it, a grub hoe is an ergonomic nightmare. It forces you to stoop at the waist, to bend and lift and chop and hack. We don't sell a grub hoe. Instead, we offer hoes designed to be used by upright gardeners. You stand straight, with knees slightly bent, and use these tools to cut weeds just beneath the surface.

Stalham Hoe

STALHAM HOE

Rather than being a chopping hoe, this is a true draw hoe. The 48" handle lets you stand erect, lessening fatigue. The head is a full 8" wide at the blade and 2½" from blade to neck; attaches easily with the screw provided. 60½" long overall. #3267 **$29.50**

COLLINEAR HOE

Eliot Coleman, a veteran truck farmer, designed this lightweight hoe for stirring the soil to cut off small weeds and to stop new ones. Its cutting edge is in line with the handle, hence collinear. 58" hoe is for gardeners under 5'6"; 64" hoe for those taller. Head is 7⅛" wide.
58" Collinear Hoe #382267 **$28**
64" Collinear Hoe #382275 **$29**

Collinear Hoe

OSCILLATING HOE

Moving back and forth, this lightweight hoe cuts weeds cleanly at the crown. Because you can stand upright and there is no chopping, no strain is put on the lower back. 48" ash handle. Two widths available.
5" Hoe #2785 **$32**
7" Hoe #2787 **$34**

Oscillating Hoe

WEEDING

Weeding need not be tedious. If you do it after a rain, most weeds come up easily. If you do it often, it's a snap. And if you bring to it Gertrude Jekyll's attitude, you'll even enjoy it. "Weeding is for me the most therapeutic of gardening chores," she wrote. "Headaches vanish and life's problems slip away as I become immersed in this world of earth and bugs, weeds and flowers."

NESS WEEDING STOOL

Comfortable, balanced, and easy to carry, this stool allows you to bend and turn freely while sitting at an optimal height for weeding and harvesting. Has a padded birch plywood seat, covered in rugged Cordura™, and a welded steel leg wide enough to remain on the soil surface. #2206 **$27.50**

RIGHT- AND LEFT-HANDED WEEDERS

For working beds and borders, this tool is indispensable. The blade is thin, very sharp, and angled to glide just beneath the surface. The slim, pointed head lets you work close to existing plants. 17" long; blade is 4¾" wide. **$12 each**
Right-Handed Weeder #2790   *Left-Handed Weeder* #2791

CRACK WEEDER

This remarkable Swiss-made weeder routs weeds out of the cracks and crannies where they love to grow. Its solid, spring-steel shaft bears a narrow, zinc-coated blade with a hooked beak. The wooden handle is comfortably shaped. 10¾" long overall; blade is ⅝" wide. #3236 **$14**

FISHTAIL WEEDER

Perfect for harvesting asparagus, this weeder also pries out deeply rooted weeds. The head is epoxy-coated steel; the handle is ash. 14" long. #2102 **$5.50**

FARMER'S WEEDER

A true grubber, this knife-shaped weeder can remove any weed in the ground. It also pulls, pierces, cuts, and pries. Carrying case has a handy belt loop. Blade is 6½" long. #2700 **$14.75**

Right-Handed Weeder   *Crack Weeder*   *Fishtail Weeder*

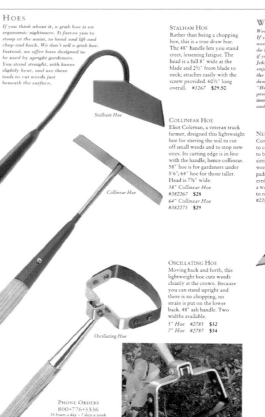

PHONE ORDERS
800•776•3336
24 hours a day – 7 days a week

18 SMITH & HAWKEN

TOOLS OF THE TRADE 19

Smith & Hawken (Garden/Tools/Furniture/Seeds)

JAPANESE FARMER PANTS

Made from lightweight cotton canvas, these pants are cool and durable. They have deep on-seam front pockets and a single rear pocket with tagua-button flap closure. Knee pockets provide a slot for foam kneepads (sold separately). Imported. Please specify size and color. **$46**
Colors: Charcoal, Oatmeal, Summer Blue
Men's Pants #70215
Sizes: S, M, L, XL
Women's Pants #70258
Sizes: XS, S, M, M-Long, L, L-Long, XL, XL-Long
Two Foam Kneepads (not shown) #4202 **$4.95**

Summer Blue

Oatmeal

PHONE ORDERS
800•776•3336
24 hours a day – 7 days a week

MEN'S GREENGOODS DENIM OVERALLS

Our overalls are built of sturdy 10-oz. cotton denim, cut large enough to fit over your clothes. Tool loops hold weeders and trowels. Pockets on bib, front hips, and back hips hold just about everything else. Stonewashed for softness and double-stitched with heavy thread for strength. Imported. S, M, L, XL; please specify. #363762 **$65**
Color: Indigo

WOMEN'S GREENGOODS CANVAS OVERALLS

The handiest work garment ever invented, overalls save you time and save your clothes. Trowel and pruners can ride in the tool loops; seed packets can hide in the many pockets (one on the bib, two in front, two in back). These overalls are made of 8-oz. cotton canvas, cut roomy and stonewashed for softness. The GreenGoods™ label on the back spells out our motto: "Make no bones about it—vegetation will save the nation." Imported. XS, S, M, L, XL; please specify. #363804 **$65**
Color: Artichoke

Men's   *Women's*

Khaki

Olive

GARDENER'S VEST

This cotton canvas vest offers lightweight transportation to small tools and assorted supplies. It's got four deep pouches in front and a two-sided pocket in back. Generous armholes and a loose fit encourage reaching, while reinforced seams and pockets retain their integrity. Imported. S, M, L, XL; please specify. (For women's sizing, please see Order Form.) #364059 **$45**
Colors: Khaki, Olive

GARDENER'S SHORTS

Your wheelbarrow may wear out before these shorts do. They're made of midweight cotton canvas, stonewashed for softness and double-stitched for longevity. Front slash pockets, back patch pockets, and tool pockets on both hips. Imported. **$45**
Colors: Khaki, Olive
Women's Shorts #371179
Sizes: 4, 6, 8, 10, 12, 14, 16, 18, 20
Men's Shorts #371039

Promotion for a high-end fashion line.

ART DIRECTORS:

Cheryl Zahniser, Carol Davidson/Nordstrom Advertising, Seattle, Washington

DESIGNER:

Carol Davidson

ILLUSTRATOR:

Helen Wong

PHOTOGRAPHER:

Dan Langley (background)

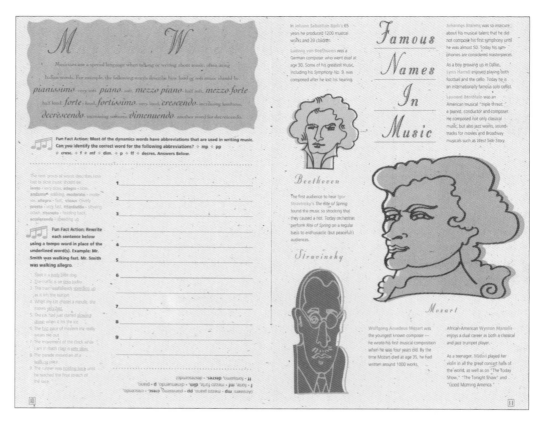

Promotion for the
orchestra's Youth Music
Education Program
sponsored by GTE.

DESIGN FIRM:

Peterson & Company,

Dallas, Texas

ART DIRECTOR/

DESIGNER: Jan Wilson

ILLUSTRATORS:

Jan Wilson, Jim Frazier,

Aletha Reppel

BUDGET: $10,000

QUANTITY: 25,000

PRINTING PROCESS:

4-color

Series of ticket sale

promotions for '93-'94

season.

DESIGN FIRM:

DiSanto Design,

Boston, Massachusetts

DESIGNER/ILLUSTRATOR:

Rose DiSanto

PRINTER:

R.R. Donnelley & Sons

BUDGET: Pro bono

Promotional mailer announcing the store's opening.

DESIGN FIRM:
m/w design inc.,
New York, New York

ART DIRECTORS:
Allison Muench,
J.P. Williams

PHOTOGRAPHER:
Geof Kern

QUANTITY: 10,000

PRINTING PROCESS:
Offset

Takashimaya, New York (Gifts/Home Furnishings/Accessories)

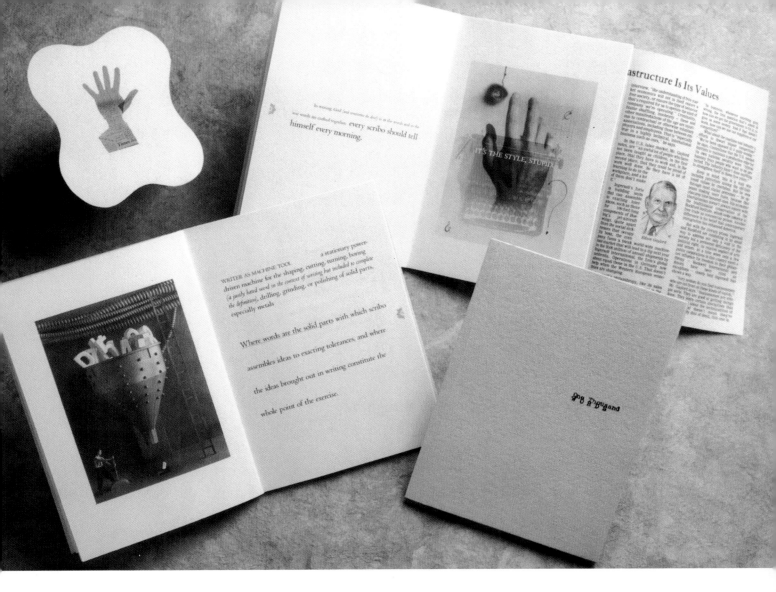

Capabilities brochure.

DESIGN FIRM: Segura, Inc.,

Chicago, Illinois

ART DIRECTOR/

DESIGNER: Carlos Segura

PHOTOGRAPHER:

Geof Kern

COPYWRITER:

John Cleland

PRINTER: Argus

BUDGET: $7500

QUANTITY: 2000

PRINTING PROCESS:

1-color

John Cleland (Technical Writing & Translating)

ORNAMENTS *In addition to the alternate swash letters, swash flourishes and ornaments were sometimes used in and around text as decoration. The Poetica ornament set consists of a series of non-alphabetic flourished designs, including spirals, knots, and ribbons, as well as a selection of pictorial designs.*

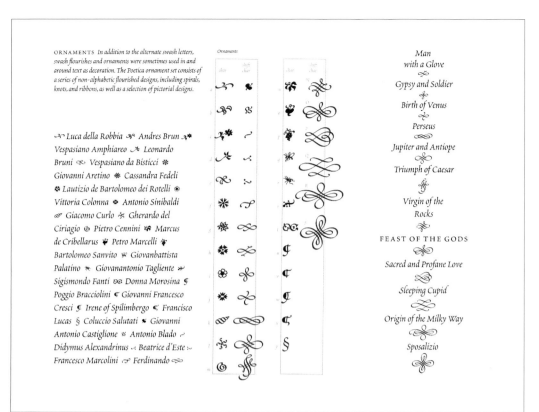

Ornaments

Luca della Robbia ✍ Andres Brun ✍
Vespasiano Amphiareo ✍ Leonardo
Bruni ✍ Vespasiano da Bisticci ✳
Giovanni Aretino ✳ Cassandra Fedeli
✿ Lautizio de Bartolomeo dei Rotelli ✿
Vittoria Colonna ❀ Antonio Sinibaldi
✍ Giacomo Curlo ✍ Gherardo del
Ciriagio ✿ Pietro Cennini ✍ Marcus
de Cribellarus ✿ Petro Marcelli ✿
Bartolomeo Sanvito ✍ Giovanbattista
Palatino ✳ Giovanantonio Tagliente ✍
Sigismondo Fanti ✍ Donna Morosina ✍
Poggio Braccilini ✍ Giovanni Francesco
Cresci ✍ Irene of Spilimbergo ✍ Francisco
Lucas § Coluccio Salutati ✿ Giovanni
Antonio Castiglione ✍ Antonio Blado ✍
Didymus Alexandrinus ✍ Beatrice d'Este ✍
Francesco Marcolini ✍ Ferdinando ✍

Man
with a Glove
✍
Gypsy and Soldier
✳
Birth of Venus
✳
Perseus
✍
Jupiter and Antiope
✍
Triumph of Caesar
✍
Virgin of the
Rocks
✍
FEAST OF THE GODS
✍
Sacred and Profane Love
✍
Sleeping Cupid
✍
Origin of the Milky Way
✍
Sposalizio
✍

Poetica

Après les choses qui sont
AFTER THE BASIC NECESSITIES OF LIFE
de première nécessité
NOTHING IS MORE PRECIOUS THAN BOOKS.
Pour la vie, rien n'est plus
FROM THE MANUEL TYPOGRAPHIQUE OF
précieux que les livres.
PIERRE SIMON FOURNIER, PARIS, 1764

Font specimen book.

ART DIRECTOR:

Laurie Szujewska/

Adobe Systems, Inc.,

Mountain View, California

DESIGNERS: James Young,

Laurie Szujewska

EDITOR: E.M. Ginger

BUDGET: $30,000

QUANTITY: 9000

PRINTING PROCESS:

Offset, lay-flat perfect

bound

Catalog for artist's Master of Fine Arts thesis exhibition.

DESIGN FIRM: Thumbnail Graphics, Hays, Kansas

ART DIRECTOR: Chaiwat Thumsujarit

DESIGNERS: Micah Walker, Dustin Smith

PRINTER: Northwestern Printers

BUDGET: $1500

QUANTITY: 250

PRINTING PROCESS: 2-color

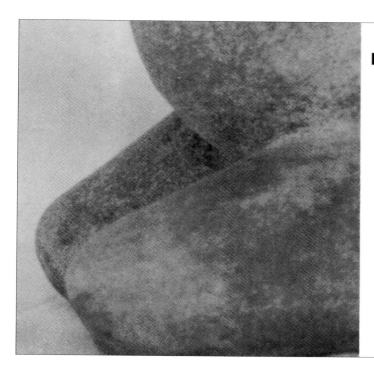

The body

container ephemeral too.

Man, in the scheme of things,

16 x 10 x 11 inches
Requium: Quiet Rest
Stoneware

lives on this earth for only a day;

looking for meaning and

purpose.

Finding

decay.

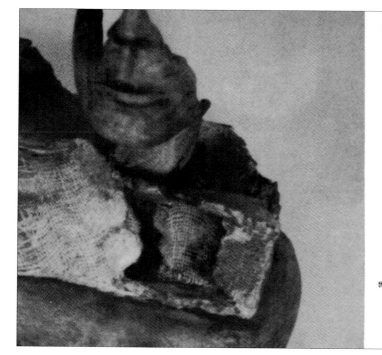

The artist

Myself.

I have learned
each sculpture I make has a voice

to speak of

the present,

the past, reflect my feelings,

my thoughts,
the way I see, life - - a struggle,

31 1/2 x 12 x 13 inches
Resignation of Thought
Stoneware

me.

Catalog.

DESIGN FIRM:

Kolodny & Rentschuler,

Vineyard Haven,

Massachusetts

ART DIRECTORS/

ILLUSTRATORS:

Carol Kolodny,

Mary Rentschler

COPYWRITER:

Elaine Sullivan

The Black Dog (Restaurant/Bakery/Store)

The score was 5-0 when Winston Churchill, spotted with his favorite colonels, exclaimed that this was Cordwain's finest hour.

Promotion for Cordwain

paper line.

DESIGN FIRM:

The Larson Group,

Rockford, Illinois

ART DIRECTOR:

Jeff Larson

DESIGNERS: Scott Dvorak,

Jeff Larson,

Keith Christianson

PRINTER:

Litho Productions

BUDGET: $55,000

QUANTITY: 35,000

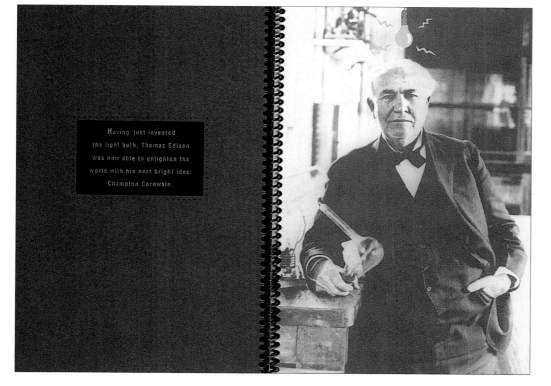

Having just invented the light bulb, Thomas Edison was now able to enlighten the world with his next bright idea: Champion Cordwain.

Champion International (Paper Manufacturer)

Promotional/capabilities
brochure.

DESIGN FIRM:

Pfeiffer + Company,

St. Louis, Missouri

ART DIRECTOR:

Jill Pfeiffer, Renee Walsh

DESIGNERS: Will Pfeiffer,

Renee Walsh

PHOTOGRAPHERS:

Ferguson-Katzman,

Mike Feher

BUDGET: $30,000

QUANTITY: 2000

PRINTING PROCESS:

Waterless printing,

300-line screen, 6-color

plus spot gloss varnish on

photos plus dull varnish

on purple solids

Reprox Printing (Waterless Printer)

Capabilities brochure.

DESIGN FIRM:

Computer Sciences,

El Segundo, California

ART DIRECTOR/

DESIGNER: Tony Salerno

PHOTO ILLUSTRATION:

Steven Hunt

COPYWRITER:

Evelyn Granacki

QUANTITY: 10,000

PRINTING PROCESS:

Lithography, 4-color plus

matte black, plus two PMS

colors plus gloss and

matte dry trap varnishes,

silver foil embossing,

diecut

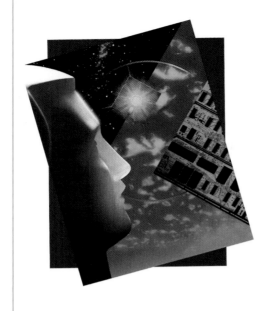

PROVEN LEADERSHIP

Computer Sciences Corporation is a leader in the science of information technology and its application for industry and government. No other company has the range of quality services we provide. CSC specializes in management consulting, systems integration and outsourcing. We offer strategic consulting services – and the critical systems development and project management skills needed to create solutions. This means we provide our clients with both strategic recommendations and a consistent framework to ensure the successful delivery of solutions on time and within budget.

Through CSC Index, our management consultancy, we help organizations transform their operations by reengineering business processes that capitalize on information technology to respond to the competitive mandates of the '90s. This reengineering approach dramatically improves order fulfillment and product development cycles while substantially reducing costs. It empowers clients to

— ONE —

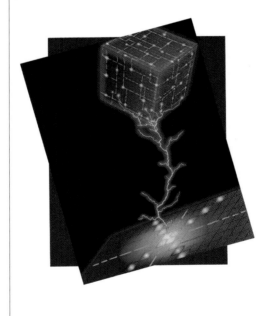

STRENGTH AND STABILITY

CSC is a company with strong financial resources, annual revenues of more than two and a half billion dollars and a staff of 30,000 employees located at over 450 offices worldwide. We understand the complex issues surrounding information technology services in today's global economy. Internationally, we provide the complete range of information technology solutions to our clients. We have major offices in Australia, Belgium, France, Germany, the Netherlands and the United Kingdom.

Providing our employees with global access to our technology databases is an important differentiator in the way we do business. We stake our reputation on staying ahead of developments in the technology arena. We hire the best people and create the proper environment for their professional growth. We surround them with opportunities to explore and apply the newest technologies and management tools by providing formal and informal networks, special classes and technology forums.

— FIVE —

Computer Sciences Corporation (Management Consulting/Outsourcing/Systems Integration)

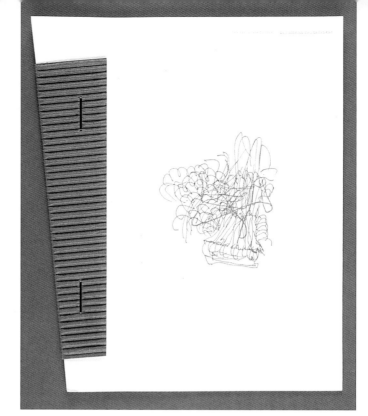

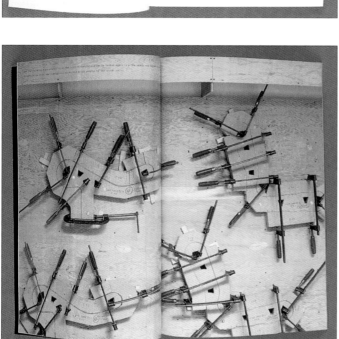

Promotion for

Quintessence Dull paper.

DESIGN FIRM:

The Kuester Group,

Minneapolis, Minnesota

ART DIRECTOR:

Kevin B. Kuester

DESIGNERS: Bob Goebel,

Kevin B. Kuester

Potlatch Corporation (Paper Manufacturer)

COPYWRITER:

David Forney

QUANTITY: 60,000

PRINTING PROCESS:

4-color

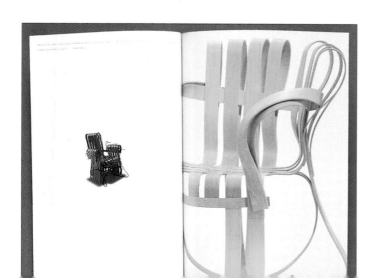

Promotion for Grandee and Renewal papers.

DESIGN FIRM: Designframe Inc., New York, New York

CREATIVE DIRECTOR: James A. Sebastian

ART DIRECTOR: Margaret Biedel

DESIGNERS: Margaret Biedel, Brian Fingeret

PHOTOGRAPHERS: Steve Cohen (left page/Tiles), Neil Selkirk (right page/Matador)

COPYWRITER: Augustine Hope

ART: Detail from *The Matador* by Pablo Picasso

PRINTER: Diversified Graphics

QUANTITY: 75,000

PRINTING PROCESS: Offset lithography

Self-promotion for

photographer.

DESIGN FIRM:

Peterson & Company,

Dallas, Texas

ART DIRECTOR/

DESIGNER:

Bryan L. Peterson

PHOTOGRAPHER:

Robb Debenport

QUANTITY: 22,000

PRINTING PROCESS:

Sheet-fed offset

lithography

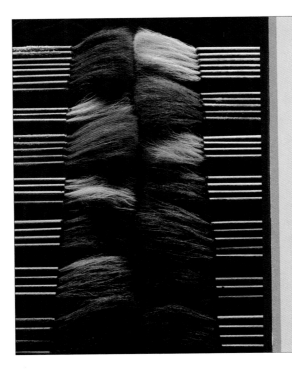

Photography may seem to be the most magical of visual techniques, but it is also the one most vulnerable to reality. Several elements must be assembled to form an image. The decisions involved come from a mental level separate from logic. Often we are asked to explain why we did something a certain way. Often we fabricate an answer to satisfy the question. We all know the concepts of visual design cannot be put into thoughts or words. Certain words, however, can symbolize ideas that we work with. Light, perspective, form, and texture are all involved. Sometimes we think about them as we work. Often we become aware of them only later in the finished piece. Other ideas like time, rhythm, and dimension may evolve in an image, but are even less explainable. Fortunately, the communication that photography brings is independent of any language process. Words may add an interpretation to the response, but visual perception moves far beyond the intellect. In these pages we have linked visual ideas with images, and even included words. Some of the connections between image, concept, and quotation are obvious. Others are indistinct; a few may or may not have explanations. But everything fit together and felt right when we were finished. A rare opportunity, a collaboration among friends. *Robb Debenport*

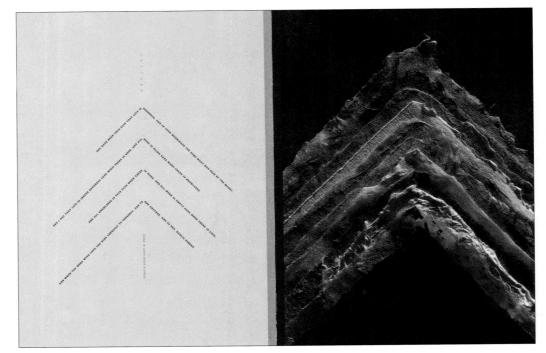

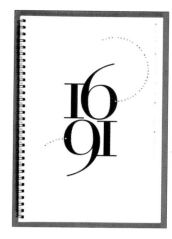

Jack **Balas**

Born in Chicago, Illinois, and lives in Boulder, Colorado. **E D U C A T I O N** MFA Northern Illinois University, 1981. BFA Northern Illinois University, 1979. **S E L E C T E D E X H I B I T I O N S** 1991 *One Person Exhibition*, Robischon Gallery, Denver, Colorado (painting & sculpture). 1991 *Rodeo in Fact and Fantasy*, 5th Stock Museum of Art, Tulsa, Oklahoma (photography). 1990 *One Person Exhibition*, Koplin Gallery, Los Angeles, California (painting). 1990 *Personal/Political: Sexuality Self-Defined*, The School of the Art Institute of Chicago, Gallery 2, Chicago, Illinois (photography). 1990 *The Right to View: Perspectives on Censorship by Gallery Artists*, Robischon Gallery, Denver, Colorado (photography). 1989 *The New Narratology—Examining the Narrative in Image/Text Art*, Artspace Annex, San Francisco, California (painting). 1989 *Books in Mind*, Arvada Center for the Arts & Humanities, Arvada, Colorado (painting). 1988 *Invitational*, Boulder Center for the Visual Arts, Boulder, Colorado (painting). 1988 *The Landscape*, Marilyn Pink Gallery, Los Angeles, California (painting). 1988 *Objects & Place*, Sibell-Wolle Galleries, University of Colorado, Boulder, Colorado (sculpture). 1988 *Visions of the American West*, 1999 Broadway Building, Denver, Colorado (painting). 1988 *Alumni Sculptors*, Chicago Gallery of Northern Illinois University (sculpture). 1987 *Coexist*, Emmanuel Gallery, Auraria Higher Education Center, Denver, Colorado (painting). 1987 *Colorado & New Mexico Photographers*, Ginny Williams Gallery, Denver, Colorado (photography). 1987 *Colorado Photographers*, Sibell-Wolle Galleries, University of Colorado, Boulder (photography). 1985 *Menagerie*, San Francisco International Airport, San Francisco, California (painting). 1985 *Gallery Artists*, Asher Faure Gallery, Los Angeles, California (painting). 1983 *Newcomers '83*, Municipal Art Gallery, Barnsdall Park, Los Angeles, California (painting). 1981 *Painting of the Month*, Los Angeles Institute of Contemporary Art, Los Angeles, California (painting). 1981 *Gallery Artists*, Roy Boyd Gallery, Chicago, Illinois (painting). 1979 *Six Sixths*, West Hubbard Gallery, Chicago, Illinois (sculpture).

Michael **Larson**

Lives in Boulder, Colorado.

E D U C A T I O N

MFA, University of Colorado, Boulder, Colorado, 1990.

BA, Humboldt State University, Arcata, California, 1987.

S E L E C T E D E X H I B I T I O N S

1992 *Chairs! Chairs! Chairs!*

Metropolitan State College of Denver

Center for the Visual Arts

Denver, Colorado

1991 *Colorado Artist Register Exhibit*

Boulder Public Library

Boulder, Colorado

1991 *Art Zone*

Jewish Community Center

Denver, Colorado

1991 *My Very Best*

Boulder Art Center

Boulder, Colorado

1991 *Anticipation '91*

Chicago International New Art Forms Exposition

Navy Pier, Chicago, Illinois

1991 *Celebrating the Art of Clean Air Show*

Foothills Art Center

Golden, Colorado

1991 *Colorado State Fair Fine Art Exhibit*

Pueblo, Colorado

1991 *9th Annual All Colorado Art Show*

Greenwood Village, Colorado

1991 *North American Sculpture Exhibition*

Foothills Art Center

Golden, Colorado

1991 *Poudre Valley Art League 30th Annual Art Exhibition*

Fort Collins, Colorado

1991 *Furniture of the 90's*

A National Juried Art Furniture Competition

Houston, Texas

1990 *Masters Thesis Show*

University of Colorado Art Galleries

University of Colorado

Boulder, Colorado

1990 *Invitational Exhibit of Colorado Ceramists*

Shwayder Art Building Gallery

University of Denver

Denver, Colorado

1990 *28th Own Your Own Art Show*

Pueblo, Colorado

1990 *8th Annual All Colorado Art Show*

Greenwood Village, Colorado

"I live in a forest environment which allows an intimate explora-
tion into nature's process. As the seasons have
passed, I have experienced changing ephemeral patterns both
dramatic and subtle, and have performed my own personal rituals: I
wrap fiber around aspen trees to capture their form and spirit, placing these
castings in the re-emerging grove, the site of their life cycle; I form a circle of
cones when drought brings an enormous pine cone fall...this circle becoming my
prayer for moisture. ■ I find strength and message in these natural objects and sites in
this mountain environment. My sculptural interventions using the indigenous and handmade paper create forms that speak of the slow process of nature...of growth, of decay and
rebirth on the land, and of our interconnectedness to this integrity. ■ An interest in the spirit
of the past has recently expanded to surrounding lands and more generally the grand landscape of the West. As I travel the West, I have been collecting sands in the tradition of the Native American medicine man gathering sands from sacred places for ritual healing. These
sands, held in vessels cast from Native American baskets, embody mythic and environmental aspects of the American West, becoming metaphors for healing and transformation.
Accompanying scrolls are documentary evidence of travels; images burned and sanded
on handmade paper speaking of the mystery of prehistoric and nature's markings
—language echoing from the past. ■ My current interest in creating installations
that recall mythic image and empathize with the earth, grows from my need
to connect with a primal consciousness—a consciousness that re-
spects and coexists with the natural environment. My belief in
the power of art itself to affect transformation
encourages my continuing search and
journey as an artist."

Mary**Ellen**Long

Promotion for Creative
Fellowship Program.
DESIGN FIRM:
Reginald Wade Richey,
Denver, Colorado
ART DIRECTOR:
Reginald Wade Richey
DESIGNER:
Karl Hirschmann
BUDGET: $4000
QUANTITY: 2000
PRINTING PROCESS:
4-color sheet-fed

Colorado Council on Arts (Fine Arts Administration)

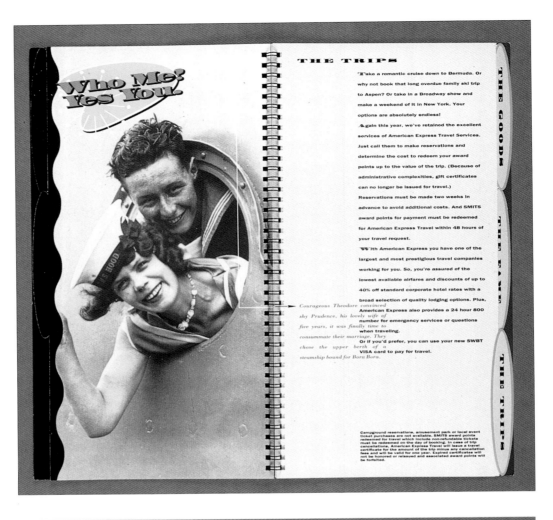

Promotion/teaser for

We're the One!

staff-incentive program.

AGENCY: Louis London,

St. Louis, Missouri

ART DIRECTOR/

DESIGNER:

Mike Binnette

Southwestern Bell (Telecommunications)

COPYWRITER: Scott Voth

BUDGET: $50,000

(complete program)

QUANTITY: 6000

PRINTING PROCESS:

4-color

Reebok Sport + Fitness sell-in brochure.

DESIGN FIRM:

DeWitt Anthony,

Northampton,

Massachusetts

ART DIRECTORS:

David Cecchi,

Dann DeWitt

DESIGNER: David Cecchi

PHOTOGRAPHERS: John

Huet, Christian Schneider,

George Fry, John Van S.

Reebok International, Ltd. (Athletic Shoes/Apparel)

PRINTER:

Universal Press

QUANTITY: 18,000

PRINTING PROCESS:

Offset lithography, black

plus three PMS colors,

4-color process over

opaque white

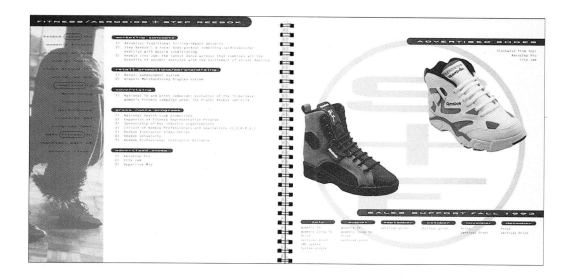

Capabilities brochure.

DESIGN FIRM:

The Hill Group,

Woodinville, Washington

DESIGNER: Chris Hill

ILLUSTRATOR:

George Y. Abe

IN A PERFECT WORLD

Imagine you are a child again entering the health care system. You don't understand

CHILDHOOD WOULD BE what illness is or why it is you're hurting. Even if you did, you probably lack the

A HAPPY TIME WITHOUT language skills to make others understand the way you feel. And even though Mom

SICKNESS OR WANT. and Dad are with you, you're lonely and you're scared.

Now take it one step further and imagine you are a caregiver trying to determine the correct course of treatment for this sick and frightened child. Think of the additional diagnostic testing that will be needed, the medical specialists that may be required. And considering the terrible vulnerability of children and how quickly their condition can deteriorate, think of the close monitoring that will be called for, the specially trained staff that is needed to provide the appropriate critical response.

Now imagine an institution where the majority of sick children you treat are the ones most gravely ill. That the complexity of cases you treat is 75 percent greater than that of pediatric programs in general care hospitals. That 24 percent of the beds in use in your hospital are designated for intensive care, compared with an 11 percent statewide average in general care hospitals. If you can imagine all this, you begin to see the challenges CHAT hospitals face each day in delivering comprehensive children's health care.

DISTRIBUTION OF BEDS

Children's hospitals continually face complex diseases which offer no simple solutions.

IF YOU WANT TO HELP

Children's hospitals in the State of Texas are facing a crisis, and it's getting worse every

SICK CHILDREN WE NEED day. The cost of providing specialized care and the continuing rise in the uninsured

YOU TO DO MORE THAN population are threatening the financial integrity of children's hospitals and

WISH US WELL. undermining their ability to provide comprehensive, accessible health care.

The plight of American health care is a complex issue legislators and policy makers will be grappling with for some time to come. With this in mind, the Children's Hospital Association of Texas would like to leave you with this heartfelt plea: When you are considering health care reform, don't forget the children. Consider the special needs of sick children. Consider the unique role children's hospitals play in meeting those needs. Remember, the world of children's hospitals is very different from that of adult patient care. Any proposed health care delivery system or reimbursement system must address these differences in order to be fair.

Through innovative treatment, service to the community, education, and breakthrough medical research, children's hospitals are reaching out to those who need us most, and ensuring the health and well-being of present and future generations. We hope you will continue to afford us that opportunity.

MEDICAID ADMISSIONS
% of Total Admissions

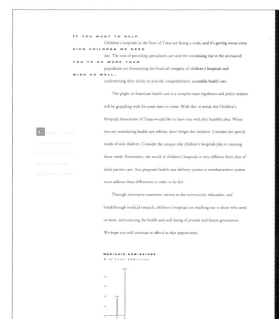

An investment in children's hospitals is an investment in the future.

Capabilities brochure.

DESIGN FIRM:

Larson Design,

Rockford, Illinois

ART DIRECTOR/

DESIGNER: Jeff Larson

ILLUSTRATOR: David Lesh

BUDGET: $45,000

QUANTITY: 5000

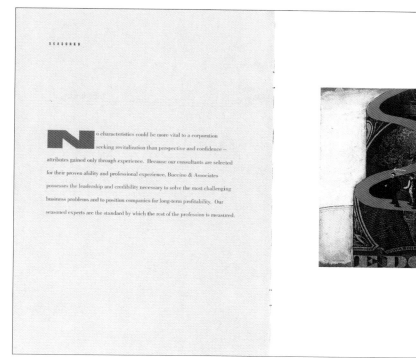

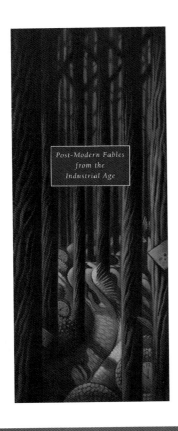

Self-promotion.

DESIGN FIRM:

Mark Anderson Design,

Palo Alto, California

ART DIRECTOR:

Tony Milner

DESIGNER: Rich Nelson

ILLUSTRATOR:

Mary Grandpré

COPYWRITER: Jon Rant

QUANTITY: 5000

PRINTING PROCESS:

Sheet-fed, 6-color, 40-inch

Heidelberg speedmaster

Bradley Printing/Midwest Lithography (Printers)

was by his peers in the industry. He talked about practically everything—except scheduling a tour through the printing plant.

Undaunted, the vigilant hawk decided to take matters into her own talons. On the way home that evening, she flew unannounced to the serpent's printing plant and slipped through an open window. Perching herself high up in the rafters, she peered down at the pressroom below. The floor was dirty and covered with scattered pallettes. A sickening odor of stale cigarette smoke hung in the air. But worst of all, instead of the half dozen 6-color sheet-fed presses the snake had told her about, all she could see was a single machine that looked as though it had been around since the days of Gutenberg himself.

The hawk's eyes then fell upon the serpent, who stood near the press talking to a young lamb client. At that moment another salesman, a rotund skunk, walked up to them and pulled the snake aside.

"What's goin' on?" the hawk

The crocodile tried to lure her into the swamp, but the deer moved on. Before too long she came upon another printer—this one staffed by a loud group of hyenas who were arguing among themselves. Finally they looked up, but the deer could get no further than her tight deadlines. "You want it when...?" the hyenas howled in disbelief, their raucous laughter ringing in the doe's ears as she hurried on her way.

Next she came upon a place called FatCat Printing. But try as she might, she couldn't get the attention of any of the plump, furry felines, who didn't even bother to listen to her. They were all too busy admiring their reflections in the windshields of their expensive foreign cars.

After this the deer encountered a zebra, who to her relief seemed much more willing to help. But as soon as the deer began to describe the bright design and art direction of her piece, the zebra cut her off. "I'm sorry," he said, "but we're a one-color printer—black on white."

And so it went. Despairing of

The Business Leadership Center was envisioned and developed by leaders of the business community, who are the primary instructors. For practical application of critical leadership skills, no other program of its kind exists in conjunction with an MBA curriculum. The Center was created by a task force composed of human resource experts and leadership trainers from such Fortune 500 companies as Xerox, JC Penney, American Airlines, Federal Express, Southwestern Bell, EDS, and AT&T, among others. The Business Leadership Center was created to address the demand from corporate America that managerial applicants come equipped to be productive and effective leaders.

Today's globally competitive corporations are no longer willing to groom managers for leadership; they expect fundamental leadership skills to be in place from day one. Student evaluations of both seminar leaders and topics allow the Center to remain on the driving edge of leadership training. The seminars presented have been tested in the business world. Moreover, the executives who conduct these seminars do so on a volunteer basis, bringing practical experience as well as enthusiasm for their areas of expertise. The Business Leadership Center offers a true reflection of the corporate environment. And it continues to be measured against the most progressive corporate standards.

Edwin L. Cox School of Business (Southern Methodist University)

Promotional brochure for the SMU Business Leadership Center.

DESIGN FIRM:

Pannell St. George,

Dallas, Texas

ART DIRECTOR/

DESIGNER: Cap Pannell

PHOTOGRAPHER:

Robb Debenport

COPYWRITER:

Carol St. George

CLIENT COORDINATOR:

Keith Pendergrass

BUDGET: $20,000 (printing)

QUANTITY: 10,000

PRINTING PROCESS:

Sheet-fed offset

To be a good manager is not enough anymore. Today's corporations demand leaders. Leaders who can coach, motivate, inspire. Leaders who can visualize what is needed in business and mobilize the resources to meet such needs. Leaders who can build teams, resolve conflicts, and create harmony from diversity. Leaders who possess not only knowledge, but skill.

The Business Leadership Center at the Edwin L. Cox School of Business was developed *by* leaders to *develop* leaders. Organized and taught by leadership training experts from some of the most progressive corporations in the world, the program builds strategic interpersonal, communication and motivational skills – the very skills required of leaders in today's globally focused corporations, yet frequently missing from the standard graduate management education.

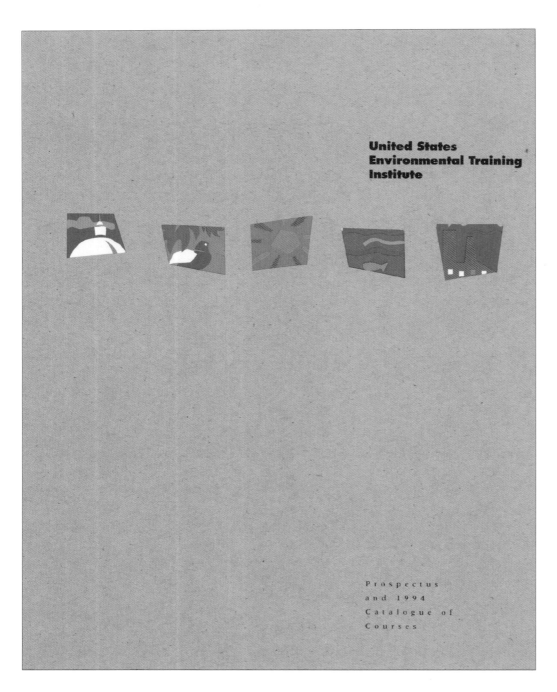

United States
Environmental Training
Institute

Prospectus
and 1994
Catalogue of
Courses

Prospectus and course catalog for a joint effort between U.S. government and environmental industry to provide training to professionals from industrializing countries in need of effective, appropriate environmental solutions.

DESIGN FIRM:
Eason Associates, Inc., Washington, DC
ART DIRECTOR/
DESIGNER: Hillary Reilly
BUDGET: $5000 (design), $15,000 (printing)
QUANTITY: 5000
PRINTING PROCESS:
5/5, four PMS colors (two fluorescent) plus black

U.S. Environmental Training Institute

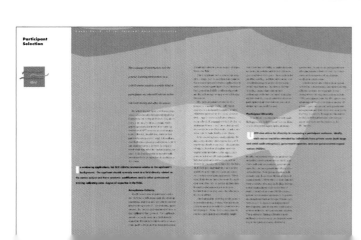

Phinney Design APPROACH

Phinney Design's creative philosophy is based on a rather straight-forward premise: Produce memorable, stand-out marketing and communications materials while delivering appropriate solutions for both our client and our client's audience.

Phinney Design can assist you in producing a diverse array of high-impact marketing materials. Projects include: identity systems and manuals, brochures, annual reports, direct mail, print collateral, packaging, signage, exhibit design, and advertising.

INVESTIGATION is one of the most important phases for creating your design and advertising plan. Initially, we research your market, and we outline any specific problems or unique circumstances that will affect primary design considerations. With this information in hand, the design criteria is developed with the client. This criteria forms the basis for your successful marketing program.

CONCEPT/DESIGN involves brainstorming ideas. We review creative concepts with you at key points in a time line, developing a consensus among all involved parties.

IMPLEMENTATION of the final design of all elements is completed with your approval. Phinney Design has no set design style. Instead, we feel that each individual account should have a look or identity all its own based on sound marketing objectives. We do, however, have a working style: Listen to the client. Analyze the possibilities. Create innovative, performance-oriented solutions.

Phinney Design

Self-promotion.

DESIGN FIRM:

Phinney Design,

Seattle, Washington

ART DIRECTORS:

Leslie Phinney,

Karl Bischoff

DESIGNERS/

ILLUSTRATORS:

Frank Zepponi,

Mike Styskal,

Adrienne Robineau

COPYWRITER:

Tyler Cartier

QUANTITY: 2500

PRINTING PROCESS:

4-color plus varnish

Fults Realty Corporation provides the security of a committed professional staff, quality service and a results-oriented attitude that clients have come to trust.

A well-orchestrated team with a solid strategy needs the principle of commitment to consistently meet its client's goals. Fults Realty Corporation stays focused on its mission of providing quality—in its professional staff, in results-oriented performance and in clear communications. It is this commitment that enables clients to fully trust that Fults Realty will establish and meet their asset enhancement goals.

COMMITMENT

COMMITTED TO PROFESSIONALISM

Just as Fults Realty establishes goals for each client's asset, the principals work with each member of the staff to establish personal goals for professional development. The firm is an Accredited Management Organization (AMO®) and has employees who hold the following designations: CCIM, CPM®, RPA® and CPA.

Their industry-certified personnel offer clients the field's top expertise. Their knowledge is amplified by participation in organizations such as IREM, BOMA, ICRS, NAIOP, SIOR and AGC.

PERFORMANCE THAT CLIENTS TRUST

From the outset of the assignment, Fults Realty establishes a sense of ownership among all team members. Clients can trust that each recommendation and decision is made with their objectives driving the process.

CLEAR, CONCISE COMMUNICATIONS

The first step in establishing a positive relationship requires listening to clients and establishing very clear expectations for all members of the Fults team. This same process of listening before taking action is consistently utilized throughout the assignment. Likewise, Fults believes in a very clear and concise flow of information to its clients, ensuring full disclosure at all times.

Commitment through professionalism, performance and communications establishes Fults Realty Corporation at the top of its field.

Fults Realty (Commercial Real Estate)

Capabilities brochure.

DESIGN FIRM:

Tom Hair Marketing Design,

Houston, Texas

ART DIRECTOR/

DESIGNER: Tom Hair

ILLUSTRATOR:

Dave Cutler

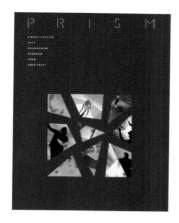

Promotion for 401K

management program,

PRISM.

DESIGN FIRM:

Sibley/Peteet Design,

Dallas, Texas

ART DIRECTOR/

DESIGNER: Don Sibley

ILLUSTRATOR:

Mick Wiggins

COPYWRITER:

John Eickmeyer

QUANTITY: 25,000

PRINTING PROCESS:

Sheet-fed offset

COMMUNICATION
EASE

*P*RISM *handles all employee communication and provides materials for you at no additional cost.*

PRISM employee communication is designed to establish and maintain maximum enrollment. We know how to market your plan to your employees successfully and how to keep them satisfied by keeping them informed.

PRISM's complete employee communication program is a major advantage for benefit managers. It saves the time and effort of meeting with employees, explaining your plan, and maintaining ongoing communications. It also saves the cost of producing information/marketing materials. We do it all as part of our standard service and for no extra compensation. First, we'll present the benefits of your 401(k) plan to your employees clearly and persuasively to assure maximum enrollment and facilitate compliance with federal regulations. Ameritrust representatives meet with your employees in face-to-face seminars to discuss the plan, show a video about the benefits of participation, and distribute customized information packets. Each packet includes a detailed plan overview, required documents, and clear descriptions of the various investment options available. There's also a handy benefit calculator, plus enrollment forms. We'll also discuss the investment options under the plan and educate participants about Trust Talk, our unique inquiry service that gives plan participants interactive, on-line access to their accounts via telephone.

DAILY
VALUATION & PROCESSING

*P*RISM *posts transactions daily to give plan participants and sponsors updates on investment performance any hour of the day.*

The PRISM methodology of recordkeeping has surpassed the traditional balance-forward system of accrual accounting. This dynamic approach is truly state-of-the-art.

PRISM's daily valuation means recordkeeping service that's second to none. It not only provides the most timely information possible but also allows same-day transfers to give participants maximum flexibility in the movement of money. Participant and plan reports are generated quickly and plan distributions are processed on a daily basis. Of course, this calls for much more sophisticated information processing, so we've enhanced and expanded our capabilities to meet the demand. As a result, our 401(k) recordkeeping will remain among the fastest, most accurate, and thorough available. Our system is also able to accommodate multiple investment options, complex vesting schedules, and share or cash accounting. What's more, we can generate reports that are customized to your needs and schedule. We handle government filings, too, and also conduct twice yearly compliance tests to make sure your plan always meets regulations. This allows us to address potential problems in a timely, effective manner. Coordinating these and all our activities on behalf of your plan is your PRISM account administrator who works in concert with a recordkeeping analyst and an assistant administrator assigned to your account.

Ameritrust (Finance)

Prospectus for an art college.

DESIGN FIRM:

Karen & Mary Designs, Detroit, Michigan

ART DIRECTORS:

Mary E. Blush, Karen Wiand

PHOTOGRAPHERS:

Heimo, Michelle Andonian

ILLUSTRATOR:

Matt LeBarre

DIRECTOR OF PUBLIC RELATIONS:

Ann Marie Aliotta

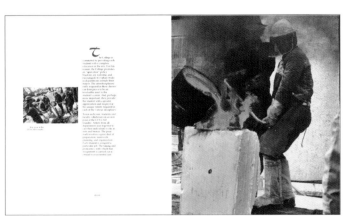

Center for Creative Studies

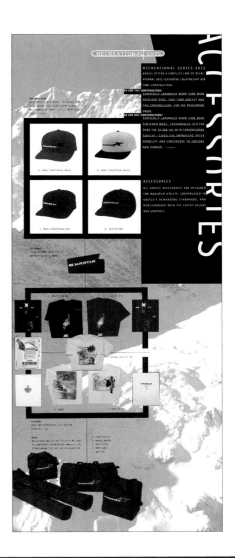

Nordica (Skiing/Sporting Goods)

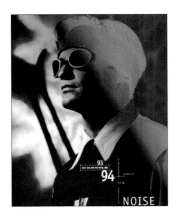

Catalog for Nordica-Kastle Ski.

DESIGN FIRM:

Jager DiPaola Kemp Design,

Burlington, Vermont

CREATIVE DIRECTOR:

Michael Jager

ART DIRECTOR/

DESIGNER: Janet Johnson

PHOTOGRAPHER:

Scott Morgan

PRODUCTION MANAGER:

David Mendelson

BUDGET: $45,000

QUANTITY: 5000 English,

1000 French

PRINTING PROCESS:

Sheet-fed offset, 4-color

plus matte varnish

(interior)

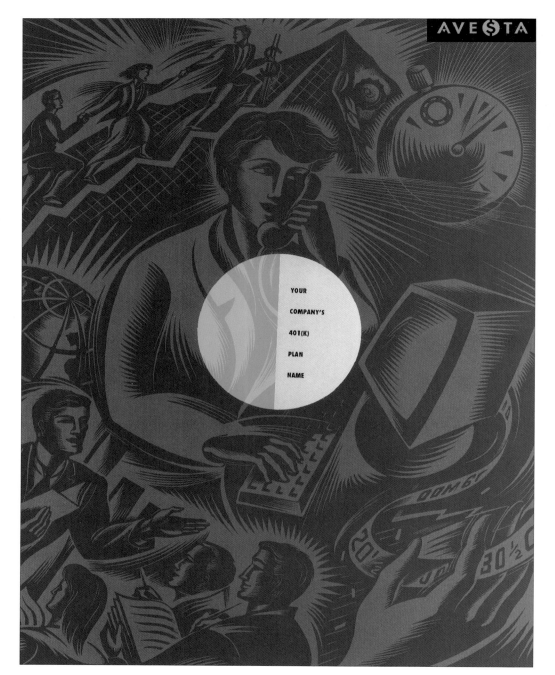

Promotion for 401K

management program,

AVE$TA

DESIGN FIRM:

Sibley/Peteet Design,

Dallas, Texas

ART DIRECTOR/

DESIGNER: Don Sibley

ILLUSTRATOR:

Cathie Bleck

QUANTITY: 25,000

PRINTING PROCESS:

Sheet-fed offset

Texas Commerce (Finance)

Annual catalog of contributions generated by participants in this arts-based forum, which brings together people from the arts, sciences, and humanities to discuss issues connecting the fields of public art, the environment, and the community.

DESIGN FIRM:

Maginnis, Inc.,

Chicago, Illinois

DESIGNER:

Rosanne Lobes

PROJECT CURATOR:

Mitchell Kane

CONCEPT:

Mitchell Kane,

Rosanne Lobes

Deleuze. Cinema I
Eisenstein Film
Form

Bourgeois Camera
Style
Faucault Interview
Gilbert-Rolfe
Immanence and
Contradiction
Before and After
the End
Place and Peterson Some
Visual Motifs of Film Noir
Baudry Ideological
Effects of the Basic
Cinematographic Apparatus
FILMS SCREENED:

Jean Vigo   L'Atalante
Sergei Eisenstein   Strike
Antonioni   Red Desert

JEREMY GILBERT-ROLFE AND COLIN GARDNER
COMPOSITION AND CONTINUITY IN FILM

Hirsch Farm

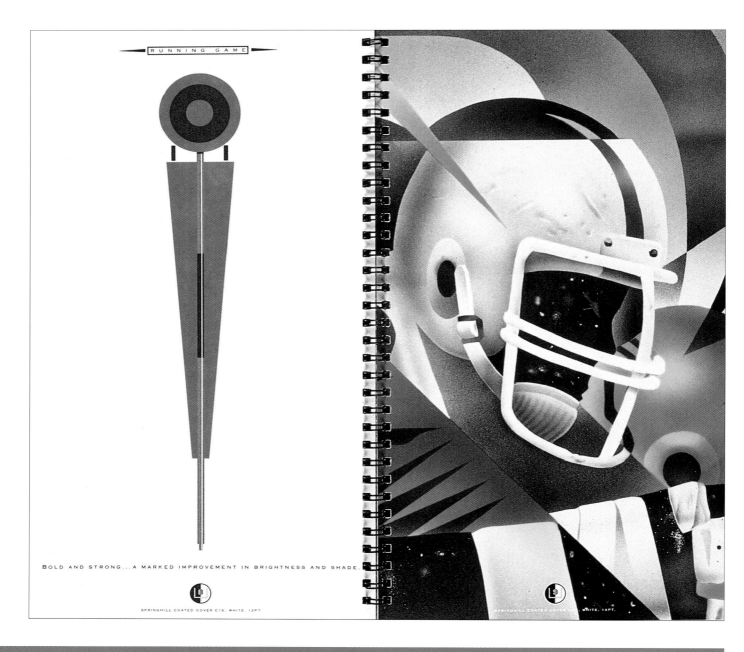

BOLD AND STRONG...A MARKED IMPROVEMENT IN BRIGHTNESS AND SHADE.

SPRINGHILL COATED COVER C1S, WHITE, 12PT.

SPRINGHILL COATED COVER C1S, WHITE, 14PT.

Promotion for Springhill
Coated Cover paper.

DESIGN FIRM:

Oden & Associates,

Memphis, Tennessee

CREATIVE DIRECTOR:

Bret Terwilleger

TYPOGRAPHER:

Jill Broadhacker

PHOTOGRAPHER:

Chip Pankey

ILLUSTRATOR:

John Mattos/

Clare Jett & Associates

COPYWRITER:

Dan Conaway

BUDGET: $90,000

QUANTITY: 40,000

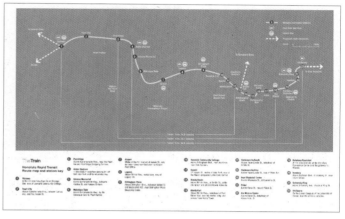

Consumer information brochure outlining the proposed Oahu Rapid Transit system.

DESIGN FIRM: Media Five, Honolulu, Hawaii

CREATIVE DIRECTOR: Lynda Black

ART DIRECTOR: Bernard Uy

DESIGNERS: Bernard Uy, Joy Matsura, Kevin Wilson

ILLUSTRATORS: Bernard Uy, Bon Hui Uy

PROJECT DIRECTOR: Peter Caderas

BUDGET: $72,000

QUANTITY: 5000

PRINTING PROCESS: Offset

THE HOUSE WON'T BE COMPLETED FOR SEVERAL MORE WEEKS.

UNFORTUNATELY, NEITHER WILL THE LAVISH BROCHURE.

UNTIL THEN, READ THIS.

STUNNING AERIAL COLOR PHOTO OF HOUSE WILL GO HERE.

Advance promotion for a lavishly renovated Chicago cottage.

DESIGN FIRM: Big Tuna, Chicago, Illinois

ART DIRECTOR/ DESIGNER/COPYWRITER: Jim Kochevar

QUANTITY: 150

PRINTING PROCESS: Xerox machine

KITCHEN AND FAMILY ROOM

The combination kitchen and family room is a spacious 17 X 19, with French doors leading to a cedar deck.

Nice tile for the kitchen floor. Red strip oak, laid diagonally, for the family room.

Custom cabinetry in maple has been ordered. Top of the line appliances, naturally.

KITCHEN SHOT: WOLFGANG PUCK OFFERS SLICE OF GOAT CHEESE PIZZA TO JULIA CHILD.

There is no obligatory powder room. Instead there is a real bathroom with a stall shower.

A laundry chute to catch stuff from the 2nd floor will be installed, too.

SECOND LEVEL

PHOTO OF POPE ADMIRING CATHEDRAL CEILING IN MASTER B.R.

3.

MASTER SUITE

The master bedroom measures 18 X 20, with peaked ceiling.

The 8 X 10 walk-in closet is bigger than many bedrooms.

The bath is 7 X 14, with whirlpool and operational skylight.

MADONNA SENSUOUSLY FROLICKING IN WHIRLPOOL.

BEDROOM #2

This one is good sized, too, measuring 18 X 14, with two Velux roof windows.

Two closets.

Original slanted ceiling lines.

Very cozy. Actually, big and cozy.

BEDROOM #3

10 X 11, with slanted high ceilings. Would make a nice child's room or office.

4.

1950 North Seminary is a single family house, built at the turn of the century, when this part of Chicago was still open fields and farmland.

Perhaps buffalo roamed through here. Perhaps not.

Perhaps bunnies and the occasional raccoon.

The building is solid masonry construction, not that mock solid veneer stuff (patooie!) being thrown up all over the neighborhood.

It was in original, unkempt, severely dilapidated, unrestored condition when we bought it two years ago. We went down to the bare bricks and completely redid the place.

Come with us now for a tour.

MAIN LEVEL

There is a new thermal leaded glass entry door with "period-correct" front porch. No anonymous calls in the middle of the night from someone chiding you about an incorrect porch. Sleep easy.

Once inside, you find a tile entry foyer and convenient guest closet.

DRAMATIC OVERHEAD SHOT OF FANCY LIVING AND DINING ROOM FLOORS TO GO HERE.

The living room floors are #1 grade red oak strip.

1.

Capabilities brochure.

DESIGN FIRM:

Devyne Design, Pasadena

California

ART DIRECTOR/

DESIGNER:

Ann MarieWhaley

DESIGNER: Edward Lum